Secret Secrets

Annette Elliot

Secret Secrets

GP

'The Families Secret Act 1960' is the euphemism I perversely bestowed upon my family code. It alludes to the secrets all families of domestic violence keep. Secrets are the silent fuel that drives domestic violence. 1960 was the year my marriage and the year my secret life of violence began.

*

With love to my three children
and with respect and admiration for all women and children who have kept 'The Families Secret Act' and suffered in silence without justice.

*

In memory of those who have lost their lives in domestic violence.

Secret Secrets
ISBN 978 1 76041 798 7
Copyright © text Annette Elliot 2019

First published 2019 by
GINNINDERRA PRESS
PO Box 3461 Port Adelaide 5015
www.ginninderrapress.com.au

Contents

Mother and me with baby cousin

Father in uniform

Photo my father carried with him during the war

Preface

'Silence is not is not golden, it's yellow, and yellow is the colour of cowards and no one in my family will be a coward.'

So said the mun who for more than thirty years abused my three children and me. He has not had the courage to acknowledge his violence, or change his abusive ways, nor has he ever apologised for his violence towards us. So here I am screwing my daunted and forlorn courage to the post to write this book about my life as I experience it. and it is scary for me to do so.

This book is about domestic violence. It is rare to find a book, an Australian book, written by an Australian historic victim of serious high-end domestic violence while their perpetrator is still living. It is risky business. So why do it? Why write about it at all?

I write to expunge my grief and then for all women who for various reasons have never been able to tell their story because, as many victims know, my story is also their story. As victims, we are all the same.

We all lose. We all lose our self-esteem, our confidence, our self-respect, our dignity. We lose our home, our assets, and we lose our family and friends. We lose children when families cast all asunder. The list goes on. And some of us even lose our lives.

We all carry grief, feel guilt, feel stupid, blame ourselves and we live in hope, we all hope thing will get better, but it very rarely does.

Many women are not aware that they are victims of domestic violence, and many are afraid to know. I write for innocent families, the voiceless children who suffer in silence, many hiding the horrendous secret within the secret, often lightly portrayed as 'child abuse'. Undisclosed paedophile fathers, and father figures whose moral depravity arc still yet to be disclosed as serious and constant offending in the domestic violence syndrome.

'Historic abuse' victims of yesteryears, often unreported until they 'recover', are those left out in the cold, many now ageing and forgotten by society and helping agencies. They are excluded from family, suffer loss of their children and have no connection to grandchildren. They are left empty, without peace and without justice.

This is my story.

1

1946–1960: Growing up

In the 1950s, every young country-reared girl seemed to want to train to become a nurse, and I was no exception. Nursing was seen as a noble, virtuous, well-protected, popular choice for girls wanting to leave home. And leaving home was not usually possible in this time when Edwardian morality was the likely faith for respectable families. Living at home under the watchful eyes of mother and father was the safe, mandated process. But leaving home was not my reason. As far back as I can remember, I was always going to be a nurse. This is the story of why that never happened for me.

*

I grew up in Port Augusta in the mid-north of South Australia, where the geographical town position sits west of the beautiful rising Flinders Ranges, a place of high peaks and deep gorges with magical colours of blues and varying shades of dusty pinks. The surrounding country is arid land devoid of tall trees or shade, low-growing mallee scrub and blue saltbush spreading across the distant horizon. It is fertile pastoral land of wheat and wool. A place of dazzling sunshine and sizzling summers, where temperatures power to exhausting heights and light rain on parched earth can instantly become a flooding plain.

In all the publicity, Port Augusta was then, and still is, called 'The Crossroads of Australia'. The local Aboriginal Adnyamathanha mob aptly called the place Cudnatta, meaning 'plenty of sand'. So true. Hot north winds blew fierce sandstorms and larrikin locals swore the pink galahs flew backwards to keep the rising sand from their eyes.

When I was a child, Port Augusta was a working port, with tall ships calling regularly at the wharf for loading the pastoral harvest for export. The wharf, constructed in 1885, with its gigantic wooden pylons and rough wooden stage, accommodated the enormous, corrugated-iron wool sheds. The wharf was a busy, bustling place, full of the activity of working men. It was also a favourite 'Tarzan of the jungle' playground for us kids. We swung from wool bale to wool bale from long ropes hung over the colossal rafters and played hide and seek as we dropped down to hide between the bales. We scooped up the spilt wheat and took pocketfuls home for the chooks. At the other end of the wharf was a wooden jetty with a small dwelling. It was built as a first-aid room for injured workers and local swimmers. It was open all summer and I spent my early teens in attendance. It was fitted out like a hospital ward, complete with iron bed, linen and hospital equipment.

Port Augusta was the main town for the surrounding sheep stations and wheat farms. The sheep grew fat on plentiful drought-resistant blue saltbush and the town was popular for its local 'saltbush mutton'. It was also a railway town, servicing the railway lines' fettlers siding camps travelling westward across the treeless, flat Nullarbor Plain and northwards to the sandy, dry, red centre. Any man who came to Port Augusta looking for work was employed in the railways or at the power station, during construction and after it was finished in the 1950s on the mudflats among the mangroves of the Spencer Gulf, where plentiful work was to be found. There was no work for women. Town women in Port Augusta were housewives.

It was a nice town and everyone knew everyone else. The men worked hard at their jobs and the women slaved in domestic drudgery. They gathered and gossiped ferociously. No one complained.

The town was geographically divided by the calm waters of Spencer

Gulf and the two red sandy sides were connected by the expansive Great Western Bridge built in 1927. The town was known as either the West-side or the East-side. The East-side was the early settlers' side, where the town's main businesses and administration centres were. The West-side was settled by the second generation of locals and was where my father and his siblings built their homes. Back then, the East-side of the town was a small settlement and the dwellings clustered around a short, main street. Everything was in walking distance.

Every Sunday, the Elliot clan met at Nana's tiny cottage and walked together to the Methodist church for morning service before returning home for Sunday lunch.

My Nana and Grandpa lived in their own small, four-roomed early-settler's cottage on the East-side. They raised their five children in that tiny house. Their cottage had once been the customs office. Maude Cottage it was called, and it was almost on the water's edge, where at low tide my Grandpa's flat-bottom fishing boats rested even-keeled on the mudflats, where I collected tiny rock crabs, and at high tide learnt to swim and catch small fish in long-necked pickle jars during our family summer holidays.

Grandpa was a sprightly six-foot Scot descendant with a quick wit, even though he couldn't read or write. He was a gentle, generous and honourable man. Before the bridge was built, Grandpa worked as a ferryman. Then he worked on the wharf loading grain and wool whenever he could, and at other times he cast out his nets and fished for a living, often generously giving loads of fish to unemployed families. In the evening he was a beachcomber, collecting Pickaxe bottles washed up on the shore, which he would sell for a penny a dozen. Each Christmas, he shared out the proceeds among his many grandchildren.

He built and repaired many of the locals' small fishing boats. All his boats were made from the locally grown trees that he and my father harvested from local bush country. He taught my father his self-taught trade of boatbuilding and Father consequently built several boats in our backyard. It was always a great day when the completed boat rolled on round logs down the sandy road between tumbleweed to be launched into the incoming high tide. Grandpa would watch with pride. He also built and raced his own self-built yacht, which he named *Reliance*, and in it he won the Coppin Cup in 1932. I proudly polished his trophy.

Nana was a pioneering woman of German descent who still used her heritage language. I used to think it funny when she greeted old Mrs Morgan, a German neighbour, with 'Guten Morgen, Frau Morgan'; the rhythm of the words sang in my ears. Nana baked her own sourdough bread in a wood oven and made soap from mutton fat in the backyard over an open fire. There was no town water and no water connected to the house. Grandpa would carry the recycled kerosene tins, made into buckets for rain water, from the tank to the house, often three times a day.

I loved my grandparents and learnt a lot from them – Nana's soft words: 'Use what you have, not what you have to have'; and Grandpa's short clipped accent: 'Waste not, want not' are both maxims that have followed me all my life and enabled me to get through many things I did later.

During the Depression years, my father began his working life for no wages – board and keep only – on his Uncle Oscar's ostrich farm in Quorn, 25 kilometres from home. This was a time when ostrich feathers still adorned fashionable English ladies' hats. Every week, he rode his bike to and from the farm, through the winding undulating Pichi Richi Pass, just north of Port Augusta, bringing home eggs and milk for his family and returning to the farm with freshly caught fish. As a young adult, he worked on the railway line as a navvy and was living in the single men's camp of tents along the rail tracks when he met my mother. He had taken a holiday in Adelaide and went to visit a school chum, Mary, who was employed at the same big house as my mother.

My mother and her siblings were raised in Adelaide and she was the middle child of four. When she was three years old, her mother died suddenly, and my mother and her slightly older brother Reginald were placed in a Catholic orphanage at Goodwood and raised there. Her eldest sister Molly was farmed out to work as a child domestic with a relative and the youngest, the baby, was passed on to another family member – we never got to know her.

Mother and her brother were dramatically unhappy. 'The nuns did terrible things to us,' she told me. They had to wear hand-me-down, faded worn-out clothes and were allowed only one set of clean underwear a week. They always smelt of pee. When she was of school age, she told me, orphans were sent to a non-Catholic school and suffered horrible taunts from the Protestant children. Mother never knew what a loving family was until she met my father.

When she turned sixteen, she left the orphanage and took up work in the big houses of the rich. On meeting my father, she agreed to marry him when, as an act of impulsive dignity, she quit her job as live-in maid to an employer who refused to replace her ragged and over-patched uniforms. 'I wore rags in the orphanage and I wasn't going to wear them when I was grown-up,' she once told me with a stubborn declaration. She cried when she realised she had no job.

'Don't worry, Valma. Marry me and come with me to Port Augusta.' Father was not the romantic kind. They married three weeks after meeting.

I do not think it was a great love affair then. Mother considered her options and decided he was a good risk. She proved to be right because he was an honourable man, a caring father, a good worker and reliable provider for us all.

My mother was a prepossessing 'superstar' housewife. She could polish and shine the furniture all day without a neatly coiffured hair falling out of place. She had beautifully manicured nails and always wore freshly laundered dresses. My father was more plebeian and, to my elegant mother's constant despair, he thought nothing of wearing a black singlet under a dazzling white shirt. 'Oh no, Frank,' she would say in frustration. He had no complaints when mother asked him to change. He was a small man, tough, strong and wiry, although a bit on the thin side. His upbringing was so very different to my mother's. He grew up in a gentle, loving family. Although they were poor, hard-working people, caught up in droughts and an economic depression, they were close, loving and caring.

As a newly wed, my mother's first home was a canvas tent, pitched among several others in a long row along the railway tracks at the Pichi Richi fettlers' camp in the Flinders Ranges. The other tents were home to single men who worked on the line. Mother told me they were respectful and full of fun. Living in her tent in the camp among the kangaroos and emus, she told me, was one of the happiest times of her life. On visits to my father's family in Port Augusta, she was welcomed and loved and she returned their love. They were the family she had never had and the one she wanted for her children.

I was born in Port Augusta three years into their marriage.

*

After the Japanese bombed Darwin at the start of the Second World War, my father took my mother and me to Adelaide. She wanted to be with her older sister for the duration of the war. Auntie Molly had given birth to a baby, two weeks before my mother. I grew through babyhood with my boy cousin and we were more like siblings. Auntie had a second baby boy, who followed us everywhere dragging his soggy wet nappy behind him. I loved him and wanted a baby brother, just like him. But my father was not around to accommodate this.

Father had enlisted with the Australian military forces and was engaged by the sixth Australian Port Operation Company to sail supply ships to the South Pacific arena. It was the company's job to accompany transport cargo on ships from one island location to another, loading and unloading necessary supplies. Fully loaded ships were sent to possible future conflict areas in the Pacific. There, the men of the Port Operation Company would unload stores and equipment onto beaches and wharves and set up supply camps for weary fighting troops as they arrived. At the end of the war in 1945, because wounded and fighting men were the first to be shipped home, my father had to continue serving, packing and clearing up the campsites, and was not free to come home for another year. Mother waited patiently with love and was proud of him.

I was almost six years old when I met my father. I was far too young to have had any memory of him when he left. All I knew of him was from his photo in his smart army uniform, complete with Australian slouch hat. My mother placed his photo alongside my bed and told me every night, 'This is your daddy – he'll be home soon.' I also had the myriad comic drawings and letters he wrote me.

My mother dealt with wartime rations and made me promises. 'When Daddy comes home…' We lived for the day Daddy would come home, when things would be different. Rations would be over and I could have as many frankfurts with tomato sauce as I wanted. I would have a school uniform and, best of all, I would have a baby brother, like my cousin had.

My father brought home many mementoes from the islands of the Pacific, but none more precious than a nurse's head veil that he had found washed up on an island beach. When I was older and learnt about the war, I wondered what poor nurse had worn it. I treasured it.

A year after his return, my sister was born, and Mother called her Dianne. Father was quite ill from malaria when he got home and he had to be treated at the repatriation hospital. When he recovered, he retrained as a specialist cobbler and made shoes for crippled and war-injured feet. He made all our shoes. Brown boots for winter and white sandals for summer. He set up in a shoe shop on Walkerville Terrace in 1947 and the shop is still a functioning shoe shop today.

*

Before my tenth birthday, we moved back to the warmer climate of Port Augusta, the home of the Elliot clan, to be reunited with Father's extended family.

Our house began as a four-roomed, timber-framed asbestos-clad, hotbox of a dwelling on the West-side. Later, to increase the size of the house, my father enclosed the back veranda. The kitchen was moved to the back of the house and next to it, close to the back door, I had a small room to myself. The kitchen became Mother's dream, with an elegant, 'posh' dining room. The house had a wood stove, without a hot water service. All the hot water came from a big kettle or a chip heater in the bathroom. The wash house was out the back and all the whites were boiled in a big copper. Washing was washed on the scrubbing board and water was carted in recycled kerosene tins from the rainwater tank twenty yards away, just like in Nana's day.

Mother loved our modest house built on a big, sandy, corner block surrounded by more sand. The house was typical of other post-war dwellings on the West-side. Building materials were in short supply and as builders and materials were not available, men built their own homes with whatever they could scrounge. Empty, recycled, square kerosene tins made buckets, or were cut open and flattened into cladding for low front fences, while big 44-gallon drums were cut open, beaten and flattened to make high back fences. Grandpa helped with building materials by collecting driftwood that had washed up onto the beach.

The long-drop lavatory was out the back – a deep hole in the sand, with a small corrugated-iron frame built over it and a wooden bench with a hole in the middle. It was my job to empty ashes from the wood stove into the pit, as ashes kept out the flies and the smell. When the hole could no longer be used, it was filled in and a fruit tree was planted over it. There was no sewage system. House water went directly onto the fruit trees. We had a lot of very productive fruit trees. We also had almonds surrounding the perimeter of our large block. Each summer, father planted watermelons, rock- and pie-melons, and our heritage tomato plants continued producing for the entire season. Our summer garden was a rich crop of chemical-free, organic food. We were close to being self-sufficient. We had pets that were well loved – a fluffy cat called Puss and a cute puppy called Furler, that grew to a ripe old age.

We had chooks and ducks, and it was my job to feed them wheat and table scraps morning and night. One morning, my sister Dianne heard a 'cheep, cheep, cheep' coming from the lavatory. A baby chick had fallen in the deep pit. Father, quick to the rescue, hammered a small platform to the end of a long rod, lowered it down through the seat hole and to our relief the fluffy yellow chick jumped on board and father pulled him to safety. We washed the chick down with the garden hose and he was as good as new.

Goannas were a constant worry, as they stole our chook eggs. One day, Mother was about to step out the back door when a goanna rushed by, its legs cycling like it was bike-riding. Hard on its heels was our little dog. 'Yap, yap,' he called as he spied the goanna. We cheered him on, 'Go, Rinny,' as he chased the poor goanna around and around the house, again and again, until Father's kindness towards all animals made him take pity on the goanna: he opened the front gate and the goanna saw its escape and bolted.

Poisonous brown snakes were many, but not so welcome, and we children were to respect them and stand clear. Whenever they appeared in the house, in the kitchen, Father would never kill them but upturned a chair like a lion-tamer in a circus and ushered them outside. It was tricky business, while we children watched, with giggles and cheers, crouched on the kitchen table.

*

Everything about me and my background was nice. I was a nice child. I had a nice home. I was from a nice family and had been given a nice, normal upbringing, with nice aunties and uncles and myriad nice cousins. I was a reasonably nice-looking child with no wonky eyes or puffy pimples. I had a few red freckles across my nose and long, thick, reddish hair with Shirley Temple ringlets. I was molly-coddled all my childhood and carefully protected from the outside world.

My Methodist church and all the church acquaintances I met every

Sunday were nice. Our Sunday evening sing-songs were comfortable and the church was the centre of my social life. I sang in the choir, did Bible studies and prepared small prayers to read during services. I played for our basketball team, the Reverend gave us our name of 'Comrades', and I attended youth activities during the week. I had hopes that, when I was a trained nurse, I would join our church in missionary work.

My life was a full circle of joy and happiness, although I was shy with strangers and did not have lots of special friends, just people I knew – and I knew everybody and they knew me. I was one of the Elliots. I was Valma's daughter, I was loved and I was happy.

I only had one special friend – Josie; we called her Jo. We were close, but I never got to know her shameful secret until we were older, much older. We were the same age and she lived one house away from my house in the same sandy street. She was an only child with respectable parents who were stricter than mine and she was often not allowed out. She rebelled, often sneaking out of the house. Jo's family was from farming people and she would drag me along to weekend farm visits. I loved the farm. We played among the sheep and went home loaded with mushrooms, fresh cream and drizzling honey just collected from the bees.

When Jo was only twelve years old, she could drive her family's beat-up old utility if her father was too intoxicated to drive home. When her father did drive, we huddled up together in the back, sitting on a pile of firewood, rugged up in blankets and covered by a huge canvas to protect us from the wind and rain as we dipped our fingers into the honey. I did not mind the rough ride. It was fun.

*

My primary school days were not part of my nice world. I had no idea what was going on in the big room. I was simply indifferent to it. It was just a place to fill in the years until I was old enough to leave school. When I grew too old for primary school, I was shuffled off to high school for a few months and then found a job at a grocery store.

*

I did not realise that I was born deaf. I was not profoundly deaf, without sound. It was just that what sound I did hear was limited and muffled. I couldn't hear what was being said in a crowded school classroom and I made up for that in other ways. I did not know that anything was missing from my world. For me, what I could hear was all there was to hear. People thought I was clever when I knew who had walked into a room even if I could not see or hear them. I could see what I could not hear. Everyone has their own particular smell, and I could smell what I could not hear. I think this caused no one to suspect I had a serious hearing impairment. I did hear sounds and that confused people.

My parents found novel ways to cope with my lack of hearing. They would announce their return home by rattling a saucepan against the kitchen sink. Some sounds were better than others. Mostly I picked the rhythm of the speech, the vibrations of footsteps or the gentle breeze as doors opened.

Neighbours thought I was strange when I heard sounds like 'da da...' I would reply, 'Mother is well, thank you' when really they were asking, 'Has your father gone fishing?' Teachers told my parents their daughter was 'intellectually retarded'. To my mind, that just meant I could not learn at school, that school was a problem, not me – I could learn other things outside of school. I did not know any other 'retarded' students, just me.

I learnt to read and write from my parents' intensive home coaching and I learnt most things I knew from them or my grandparents. And for some unknown reason, I was quick at maths and could sort shillings from pounds in a flash. I knew I was different, as I never passed any school exams. A new teacher introduced a 'good merit' system. I scored well and moved from one class to the next because I acquired lots of 'good merit' points; good merit points for my nice painting, for being the best basketball player, because I could run fast and because I was a 'good girl'. 'Good girl,' the teacher would say, and I got another merit point. I had no idea what other kids were doing but I worked hard on getting 'good merit' points. It was not easy being nice all the time to get my 'good merits'. I had to smile a lot and be an all-round 'good girl' and I had lots of 'good merit' points to prove it. I was polite and never got into trouble like some of the girls in our town. I always did what my mother told me to do. I knew other mothers gossiped about other mothers' daughters but not about me. I gave no reason to be gossiped about. I could not be clever but I could be a nice 'good girl' and my mother was happy with me.

A few weeks close to my thirteenth birthday, a new teacher arrived from Adelaide to take over the small three-roomed school on the West-side of Port Augusta. He arranged for me to see an Education Department audiologist in Adelaide. After a medical and audio test, I was told that I was deaf and they offered me a hearing aid.

'No! I'm not deaf! I'm retarded,' I told him. 'No, thank you. I do not want a hearing aid.' If I had a hearing aid, people might think I was deaf and it would not be nice for my parents to have a deaf child. I would have none of that. Being deaf meant that I wouldn't be able to be a nurse. Besides, I argued, I could hear the beeps of the test machine and the tramcars clattering past. I did not believe I had failed the hearing test. The testers had cheated by speaking quietly behind my back, but I was told that I had not heard what was being said, and I retorted that no one ever speaks to you behind your back and that when people talked to me slowly in front of me, I could always make out the gist of what they were saying, or at least I thought I did.

'You *are* deaf,' he insisted, leaning in close to my face to make sure I heard what he said.

'No, no,' I cried tearfully. I did not want to be deaf. I wanted to pass the health check and I wanted to be a nurse.

The man was kind and told me I could be a nurse if I had a hearing aid but without one I couldn't.

'Oh, well, that's different then. In that case…'

My parents were pleased that I had accepted the hearing aid, but people would stop and offer sympathy to my mother.

'Oh, Mrs Elliot, I am so sorry your poor Annette has to have a hearing aid.'

'Oh no! Not at all. We're pleased. Now she can hear. Now we know what's really wrong with her.'

And I was happy that my parents were happy with me because, in the long run, that was all that mattered to me. In time, I got over the worry and discomfort of having to wear the hearing aid. It was heavy, big and bulky with a long cord and I had to carry it around in my little trainer bra. The hearing aid caused me a lot of stress. People expected a lot from me now and thought I would hear everything, but it was merely an aid, that was all. It did not offer perfect hearing. It burped and buzzed and at times overshadowed the voices.

When people noticed the hearing aid, they would shout at me and that was not good either. I still did not always know what people were talking about, but it did open up new sounds to me. I still lived in my own happy, uncomplicated blend of mystic fusion.

'What's that noise?' I would say to my friend Jo.

'What noise?' she would reply.

'I can hear a noise but I don't know what it is.'

Years later, I learnt my deafness was hereditary; older great-aunties and some of my cousins also had the same problem and the condition could pass from generation to generation.

It took me years to identify what noise went with what. Chickens' chirping went with chickens and puppies' whimpering went with puppies, I had not heard the sweet music of wind through the leaves of swaying trees nor did I know that water splashing over rocks could give a rhythm of peaceful pleasure.

*

There was never any doubt in my mind that at some time I would become a nurse, and my opportunity came sooner than expected.

When I turned twelve, before I had the hearing aid, I joined the St

John Ambulance Association as a junior cadet. The face-to-face contact with instructors gave new meaning to my learning, such that my parents were both astounded and confused. Their 'intellectually retarded' child who failed at school excelled in all matters of junior first aid and I passed the exams with flying colours. My high achievements made me popular, just like the clever kids at school. Mr Knight, our instructor and organiser of the association, took great care that my 'retard' deafness did not exclude me at any time.

Mr Knight and his family settled in our mid-north town after they had lost their home and all their belongings in the wartime bombing blitz in London. Mr Knight had been a medical orderly and had helped run medical aid stations. He told us the fierce molten fires had caused awful burns and that burning skin would bake flour hard if you put it on open wounds. So his first advice to us in his opening every tutorial was never to put flour on a burn. My Nana would put butter on burns but it seems during wartime many others would dust a burn with baking flour. Mr Knight explained that flour would cause infection and then it had to be removed piece by tiny piece with tweezers that pulled away layers of flesh, the casualties screamed in agony. That had been his job and he relived the horror of the painful creams each week and he cried tears as he would repeat, 'Never put flour on a burn.'

I continued with St John Ambulance volunteering and provided community service at many town functions and sporting events. My tuition in first aid was extensive and covered training in the event of accidents where I could take control if there was no one more capable around.

*

I was several months past my thirteenth birthday and getting used to my hearing aid, when we were given home nursing instructions as well as first aid. Home Nursing was a course for girls only and was conducted by Sister Jones. She was also a Londoner who had left after the war. Our instruction classes were conducted in the small first aid room at the end of the jetty on the foreshore. Sister Jones gave me and the other girl's copies of Sister Betty Jeffries's book *White Coolies*, which told of the experiences of nurses during the Pacific war with the Japanese and how they were captured and many shot on the beaches. (Father never spoke about the war.) She herself had been a prisoner of war and had watched nurses die from being shot, from starvation and from inhumane cruelty. However, we would-be nurses saw past the cruelty and horrors of faraway war; we saw adventure and heroism, and we wanted to be just like Sister Jeffries.

At the nursing classes, we girls were taught to give injections, to clean and dress wounds, control infection with barrier nursing methods, test urine and many other duties carried out by first-year training nurses of those days. We idealistic young country girls were in heaven. For us, a nursing career was the ultimate 'girl's own adventure'.

Matron Fitzner, a tall, stern, upright woman, in charge of nursing staff and training at the local hospital, regularly tested us on our nursing abilities and we all passed brilliantly. She told us we would all be good nurses. Matron invited me to come and talk with her and told me she would have a training place for me as soon as I turned eighteen – I could hardly wait. Meanwhile, we could have our St John 'nurse' uniforms: white dresses, a black cape and black felt hat, black stockings and black shoes.

Of course, we fifteen- and sixteen-year-old 'home nurses' jumped at the chance when we were asked by Matron to help out at the hospital on weekends and at Christmas. Our own Sister Jones was ever so proud of Matron's confidence in us. That Christmas, Matron wanted all her hospital nurses to have Christmas lunch together and so she asked us home nurses to look after the wards for two hours while they were absent, in the big hospital nurses' dining room.

We 'nurses' had time to have our head veils made. I already had mine! The one my father gave me on returning from the war. I was so proud of my veil. As a small child, it had been my dress-up play-nurse uniform and now I was to wear it for real.

We reported for duty to the ward sister to be given instructions for what we were supposed to do for the afternoon. It was Nurse Elliot and Nurse Carlton reporting for duty in the long, single room which was the women's ward! When the nurses all left to join matron, we home nurses began work.

We puffed up pillows, tidied already tidy beds and polished already sparkling bedside cabinets that did not need any more sparkling. We straightened out the fresh flowers in their perfect vases. We filled water jugs. Then we did it all over again. The patients were suitably harassed during their rest period and the two hours passed quickly; our sense of self-satisfaction reigned high. When the nurses returned from Christmas lunch, all the patients' pillows faced the correct direction, the openings facing away from the door, the water jugs were full, the bedside cabinets shone brightly, just as Matron insisted. No patient had had to wait a moment for a bedpan that day.

Sister Jones, wearing her smart English wartime army-style nurse's uniform, always went to the local Anzac Day memorial services. She encouraged us girls to accompany her and we proudly stood beside her, all of us in our home nurses' white linen dress uniforms, shiny black shoes, black stockings and black felt hats. We looked out of place among the crowd of returned solders in their odd assortment of old and worn khakis. We were frowned upon by the dominant 'old men'. Anzac Day, we were told, was for soldiers, not skinny kids dressed up like nurses, so we were relegated to the back of the gathered crowd away from the soldiers. But we 'remembered them' and, especially, we thought of the wartime nurses Sister Betty Jeffries wrote about.

*

A few weeks before my fourteenth birthday, a vacancy came up in our local grocery store. My father permitted me to leave school and so I began work. Within weeks of my employment, I arrived outside the shop at eight-thirty in the morning, as I usually did, waiting for Mr Woodford to open the door. I was surprised to see a small man dressed in a smart suit arrive on his bicycle. He said he was from the union and he asked me for five shillings to join. I was horrified. Give him five whole shillings and he would give me nothing in my hand? I would have none of that. The shop door opened and I scurried inside, glad I had a narrow escape.

When I told my unsympathetic father of the mean man who wanted my money for nothing, he was cross with me. 'Why do you think Mr Young, the owner, gives you two pounds six shillings a week? Do you think he likes you? No! You get two pounds six shillings a week because the union fought for your wage. You join the union, girl, and as long as you're working and earn a wage, you stay with the union.'

I joined the Shop Assistants' Union.

I didn't like the grocery store, where I was the only girl. The other two employees were married men, with daughters younger than me. One man rode his bicycle around the West-side and collected the orders and the other drove the truck that delivered the groceries I had packed into small wooden crates. The older man was constantly rude to me, sang dirty ditties to make me blush and often grabbed me and briefly held me close, always laughing and making jokes, but I was constantly on guard and always felt uncomfortable.

A year later, I accepted employment in the new Coles store, selling lollies. There, the assistant manager, whose job it was to 'walk the floor', was also a girl grabber. He would put his hands tightly on our hips and grab us towards his body as he passes the narrow space behind the counter. He would grab our back bra straps out and let go with a snap, snap, then laugh. One girl turned and slapped his face; she was instantly dismissed. Sexual harassment had not been given a name in those days and the incident merely told the other women and girls working there to simply grin and bear the 'male privilege' behaviour and not to complain.

*

Every small town has its gossips. One of the West-side's gossips was a Mrs Glen, who lived up the road from us. She was a real busybody. She was always out the front of her place attending to her garden and she kept a keen lookout for someone to stop and exchange confabulations. She had a daughter who was two or three years older than me and who worked at the local doctor's surgery. One day, as I was passing her house, the daughter called to me; she told me my mother would be having a baby in October, a couple of months after my fifteenth birthday. I was astounded. My mother, having a baby? I told my mother what she had said. My noble-minded mother, normally cool and ladylike, was furious. She had not yet told my father and was herself unsure when her baby would be born. She flew over to the surgery with me following close behind and pounced upon Miss Glen with a thorough tongue-lashing with all the ladylike aplomb and dignity she could muster. That was the only time I ever saw my mother indulge in fury.

Mother was indeed pregnant. Nana died later that year and when my baby sister arrived in October the same year, Mother named her after Nana.

*

Just before I turned sixteen, our local church minister told me he knew the matron of a children's hospital annexe, a place for polio convalescing children in Adelaide, and he gave me an introduction via an exchange of letters. I was accepted to work as a nurse. I was ecstatic and acquired real nurse's uniform. At last I would begin my dream. I was disappointed when I discovered we 'nurses' were little more than domestics, giving enemas, fetching bedpans and cleaning up distressed kids spew. It was demanding work and I was very young and timid and I had never been away from my mother and father. I could not cope with the jesting and teasing of the more assertive mature city girls. I returned home to my family after only a few weeks and began work back at the Coles store.

*

I was only a few months into my sixteenth year when I came face to face with my future husband, although I didn't know it at the time, at our local Friday-night 'sociable'.

The sociable was a regular meet-and-greet event for young teenagers and doubled as ballroom dancing classes for beginners. I had bought myself a dazzling, ballerina-length, organza dress especially for all the dancing occasions. I loved wearing it for dancing. There were no real dance teachers at these evenings. Teenagers simply stumbled and fumbled around the floor until they got the hang of it. It was a case of follow whoever was in front of you. Sometimes, married couples might lead the way, and my parents contributed.

The sociable was held in the rusty old 1930s corrugated-iron Church of England Sunday school hall, just a short walk from our house. Entry cost one shilling and sixpence. It was run by the women of the church ladies' auxiliary and they provided keen, hawk-eyed supervision: no lingering by couples outside was allowed. No smoking and no drinking alcohol, no fights or bad language. It was a very respectable affair. Tall and wiry Mr Jones, the shoe shop proprietor, played the piano and he collected a band of old musicians who could belt out a good waltz or two. He also played the organ at our church and saw to it that everyone, but especially the boys, behaved themselves. Country women are renowned for their bountiful, delicious suppers and our women provided hot chocolate and pots of tea along with homemade sponge cakes for our supper.

My father usually took me to the sociable but this week he was repairing his fishing nets and so did not accompany me to the dance. My friend Jo came with me. Jo was one month younger than me. She was a serious girl and always seemed to me to be unhappy. She was taller than me and had pretty, long, blonde hair. She wore lots of make-up and looked older. We had been best friends since I arrived at the school.

At the sociable that night were Mack and his friend Jock; they met while living in the railways workers' 'single men's accommodation, not a savoury place for young teenage girls. They were not teenagers like us but itinerant 'blow-in blokes' and no one I knew, knew them. They smoked rolled tobacco and smelt like the hotel I walked past on my way to work. To me, they looked knockabout and shabby. They had tried (and failed) to dress 50s rock-and-roll style; their 'ducktail' haircuts were overgrown, shoes were scruffy down at heel and needed polish, and they looked out of place at our teenage sociable.

Jo was an attractive teenager; she was confident with boys and they flocked to her, and this night the two blow-ins homed in on Jo. Shy and reserved, I did my best to ignore them, but Jo was impressed that Jock was older, not a silly, trembling teenager. He had come from Scotland as one of the Barnardo boys years earlier and, to Jo, he seemed like an exciting overseas lad. Meanwhile, I was not at all keen on the attention I received from Mack. He hung around close to me all night and when the evening ended around nine o'clock, Jo encouraged both men to walk home with us.

I was disgruntled, and haughtily bolted out of the hall door and charged ahead, leading the way. Mack caught up and Jo lagged with Jock. Our houses were at the end of the sandy street, which was little more than a dirt track, and there were no street lights. It was very dark.

I hurried to my front gate, where my bike was hanging over the half-sized kerosene-tin-clad fence and Mack nearly tripped over it in the dark. I giggled to myself, 'What a goose.'

When I stopped at the gate to say goodnight, he asked me if he could take me to the pictures the next night.

'No,' I said with an indignant air. 'I was going with Jo,' and then I offered a polite handshake, just as my mother had taught me. I thanked him for walking me home – thankful, that is, that the walk was over, and quickly scuttled inside.

On Saturday night, Jo and I caught the seven o'clock bus to the main street. It stopped outside the library just short of the picture theatre. Jo was lingering after we stepped off the bus and then suddenly looked ahead and smiled. I was annoyed to find the two chaps waiting for us outside the theatre. Jo had not told me that she had agreed to meet Jock outside. And there was Mack standing beside him, smiling like a Cheshire cat. I refused to let them think I would sit with them, and raced to buy our tickets. I was not happy that they were there, nor that Mack was being so smart about it. But at interval, Jo was happy to meet them in the foyer and I grudgingly stayed close. I did gobble their offering of very expensive and enticing chocolates, wrapped in bright fancy paper, the like of which I had never seen before.

My mother and Jo's mother went to the morning service at our tiny, makeshift church on the West-side, one street away from our homes, but Jo and I went to the main church on the East-side on Sunday nights because we liked the social interactions with the younger set.

The Sunday after the pictures, we were sitting in our pew, in our regular place towards the back of the church, when I was irritated to see the chaps, the two ruffians, loudly reciting the Lord's Prayer. When the collection plate went around, Mack turned and flashed a ten-shilling note at us. 'Well!' I thought. 'Perhaps they're not so bad after all: expensive chocolates, the Lord's Prayer and ten shillings.'

After the service, our young Reverend, always polite and pleased to see newcomers, even scruffy ones, invited them both to come to our regular Sunday-night sing-song for us teenagers. It was held at the residence of the town mayor, who was also a member of parliament. His wife played the piano and we all sang popular, catchy Methodist hymns and other uplifting, inspirational John Wesley songs.

With the two chaps' persistence and Jo's enthusiasm to keep Jock interested, it was inevitable that the four of us would end up going to the pictures the following Saturday. Despite my reservations, we continued for some time to go out together in what must have appeared to others as two couples. Jo wanted Jock's attention, but it was not socially acceptable to be seen out alone with an older man and a stranger to the town. It would fuel malicious gossip and so my company was necessary. I was unsure who was chaperoning whom.

The two men eventually met our respective parents and Mack was respectful, charming and generous. He brought flowers for my mother (he picked them from outside the fence of Mrs Glen the gossip's house), ingratiating himself with crafty persuasive flattery. I was peeved. Mack was clever enough to show my father that he was interested in net fishing and boats and was a willing helper in maintaining the nets. Before long, he was a regular at our house, always with more presents for my mother. He was from Sydney and six years older than me, although at the time he seemed much older in my eyes.

I later learned he was from a fractured, blended family. His mother had been divorced once, and was a war widow before she married his father. She had three children from those marriages and in her third marriage she had two more children – Mack and his sister. His father had also been married before and brought a child to be raised by his mother. His father was a veteran of Gallipoli and suffered all his life from injuries. He was quick with a pencil and did tote for the local bookmaker.

It was a particularly difficult time for men and women. Unlike most families living in their street, his father was in regular employment. His mother, burdened with earlier economic depression, war, birthing, and struggling to raise her many children, often provided meals for the neighbours. She was a good woman who cared for some of the neighbourhood brats of Woolloomooloo when their battered and weary mothers were suffering from backyard abortions. Many children were left motherless because of those illegal abortions in those days, his mother once told me, and she herself was no stranger to violence; when her children were grown and left home, she felt no sorrow when her husband died suddenly.

Jo's mother was a bit miffed about Jock, but she was too gracious and full of Christian goodwill to say anything untoward. She showered him with motherly attention. Jo's dad was a country farm boy, who had lost the family farm to his older brothers and he was not overly communicative, so he offered no comments. As long as Jock, who was Catholic-reared, went to our Methodist church and had Mack nearby, it was all okay. Thereafter, they were regulars at Jo's place.

*

My attitude took a big shift when Mack told me both his sisters were trained nurses and, more to the point, that he had spent many days and weeks at a time tutoring them from their textbooks as they prepared for their general nurse and midwifery exams. I was captivated by his knowledge of nursing and the stories he told me of the adventures he shared with his sisters and their fellow nursing mates. He was learned, funny and entertaining. I found he was generous and a willing, helpful man. He often bought small gifts for me and he charmed my mother, who was intelligent, with wide interest, well-read and more cultured than her peers. She was starved for intellectual company in our town and Mack brought her varied conversation and many books that she liked to read. He was also a reader and spent time discussing books he and she had read. He won her over, and that made things difficult for me.

I was still attending St John's and my home nursing lectures. Just to make sure Mack remained aware of my future intentions, my talks with him were all about my plans to be a nurse. Then one day he gave me a book written about Matron Edna Shaw and Crown Street Women's Hospital, a famous Sydney training maternity hospital, and told me his sisters had done midwifery training under Matron Edna Shaw. With exaggerated animation, he demonstrated how Matron

Shaw would execute her elite professionalism. He was a real raconteur, a good mimic, and made us all laugh. I was mesmerised and could not get enough of the antics and stories of his sisters. In those days, nurses lived on site at the hospital and Matron took responsibility to ensure her nurses did not stay out late at night. But they often did, and their daring escapades and flirting without being caught out kept me transfixed and I had expectations that I would be one of them soon.

*

My father arranged employment for Mack on the building construction site of the new power station being built at the Spencer Gulf. He thus became one of my father's workmates and a constant visitor at our house. My father also took Mack on his weekend fishing expeditions, as it was father's regular winter weekend occupation. Mack continued helping him repair the nets and the boat engine.

My father trusted him with the family car and one Sunday, Mack drove me to a small country town about 40 miles south of Port Augusta, to their Methodist harvest festival thanksgiving service. It was what we did back then – visit another town's special church occasions. Often, the youth ran the service and we felt it proper that the youth of our town should attend and be supportive.

On the way home, I became worried when Mack drove off the highway onto a dirt track and parked out of sight of the road. He tried to pull my dress up and my pants down. I jumped out of the car and would not get back in. I stood in the shade of an acacia and refused to get back into the car. Eventually he pleaded, saying Father would be getting worried if we were not back soon.

Mack was becoming a pest, waiting for me after work, coming to the house in the evenings and showing up at our teenage dances, then insisting he walk home with me. I was becoming more annoyed by him.

Another time, Father was away fishing and Mother was next door visiting Jo's mother, when I came out of the bathroom with just a towel around me. He was sitting on my bed. I was stunned. Only Jo ever came into my bedroom, for girly talks. Bedrooms were completely off-limits to everyone else. I screamed and yelled and told him to get out, that he shouldn't be there. He lingered and only swaggered out with a smirk on his face, when I told him Mother was coming back from next door.

One weekend, my parents were at a football match and I was home alone. I did not hear Mack walk into the house through the open back door – when I was alone, I often did not wear my hearing aid. I was lying on my bed reading a comic book and he walked boldly into my bedroom.

I looked up in fright. 'Get out of my room,' I said.

He just laughed at me and straight away sat on my bed. Before I could sit up, he placed a hand on my chest, pressing me down. He was calm, unhurried, and sneaked the other hand into my shorts. I did not know what he was doing. Then he was touching my private parts, forcing his fingers between my legs.

I pulled his hand out and rolled to one side. I drew my knees up to my chin and pushed myself to the far corner away from him. 'I'll tell my father on you, go away,' I shouted. I sat curled up into a ball and pulled my pillow into my arms against my knees and held on tight.

Then he just left.

Our town was considered safe and no one locked their doors in those days. After the incident, I asked Father to put a lock on my bedroom door. He did, but never asked me why.

*

I liked working at Coles on the confectionery counter. I was paid an extra five shillings to wash my two pink work uniforms. One day, I was caught eating lollies and they moved me to the counter selling glassware. There, I also had to paste up the price signs. I felt I had

33

advancement, sitting in the tiny ticket office. A new boy joined the store and it was his job to deliver the heavy glassware for me and to collect the signs I had made. His name was Kevin and he was a junior storeman, my age. During the day, we talked a lot. He was well-dressed, gentle and had nice manners. He was English and his family was one of hundreds of young families who migrated to South Australia in the 1950s. His family lived in the new area of Elizabeth, north of Adelaide, and he had come to our town for work. We went to the pictures together and often went for walks along the beach, or went to the new Caltex service station for hot chips and a cold Coke.

One night, after the store had closed, Mack watched me leave through the front door and waited for Kevin to come out. Mack followed him. I was at home with my family when a friend of my fathers, came running to our house shouting that Mack had been arrested for fighting in a laneway off the main street. Father went to the police station and eventually brought Mack back to our place. Mack had bashed Kevin badly. He made Kevin agree that they were fighting over the Australia versus England test cricket match. Father agreed to assist them both to leave the police station without further ado. He did not want his innocent daughter's name to be related to the incident. Fighting and police were not things my family ever wanted to be associated with. It spelled shame and all things undesirable.

Next day at work, Kevin was so badly injured his eyes were bulging black and blue. He was so damaged that he could not leave the storeroom to go to the front of the store and he struggled all day. He was distraught and told me that he could not see me any more. I was very disappointed when he left town a few days later. The Coles manager called me into his office and told me my 'boyfriend' (meaning Mack) was barred from the store. Mack was cocky and ignored my warning not to come bother me at the store.

Thereafter, I was no longer treated well by management and not much later I was given notice, without the wages owed me. My father sent me to the union representative, who spoke to the Coles manager and they gave me an extra week's pay, as well as the money they owed me. I was glad to have paid my five shillings union membership.

I went to work in my father's friend's fish shop.

*

As a family, our very hot days were spent in the shady western outside of the house. We would lounge beneath the thick grapevines where a water hose attached to a sprinkler sprayed a light, showery mist over the vines and the soft breeze would cool the shady spot. There was no air conditioning in those days and we kept cool as best we could. During the hot summer nights, our timber-framed, asbestos-clad house was a furnace. When the sun went down and the temperature eased, we sometimes cooked chops or fish, barbecue-style, outside, and, in picnic fashion, ate dinner on our blanket on the back lawn. We ate outside, we slept outside. Some families had permanent beds, kitchen tables and chairs outside, but not us. Mother thought they were crude. Outside, under the canopy of grapevine trellis and water spray, was how most families coped during extreme summers.

As a family, when the sun went down, we were together this particular hot night, sitting on a blanket spread on the cool lawn. We had finished our picnic tea when Mack called by. He had bought a big carton of ice cream for us all and we rushed to dish it out before it melted. He stayed and talked to Father for a while and then Father said we were all to go to bed and it was time for Mack to leave. He left while my parents and I were packing up.

My parents and sisters slept inside that night but I settled to sleep on the blanket with my pillow and sheet, with a mosquito net over me like a tent. I left my hearing aid inside my bedroom.

I was sleeping soundly when I woke up suddenly to find I could not move my legs or sit up. Something was holding me down. My short pyjama pants and my sanitary belt and menstrual-bloodstained napkin were around my ankles. I was shackled and could not move.

Dazed from my sudden awakening, I tried to sit up, but horror, oh horror! The 'something' was Mack lying on top of me.

'What are you doing?' I cried out. 'What are you doing? Get off me, get off me!' I screamed over and over again. It took me some time to realise what was happening, and then I knew he was raping me. I fought back, trying to push him off me, it was useless. My arms were flapping about like a baby chick trying to fly. I screamed at him to get off me! Get off me! Get off me! There was no one to hear me in that dark isolated backyard in the dark black street.

'I'll tell my father on you,' I said over and over again. 'I'll tell my father, I'll tell my father,' like a pouting belligerent child – as the child I was. I protested until he cupped his hand across my mouth and held it down tight.

His face close to my ear, he hissed, 'Shut up. No one can hear you. Now you're used goods. No one will want you. You're nothing, you're nothing, you're mine. No one loves you more than me, and you can tell that kid from Coles to piss off. Stop snivelling, you're not hurt, and now you'll have to marry me.'

My thoughts raced to my mother. Oh no, my poor mother. I heard her voice in my head: 'Nice girls don't… Only bad girls have sex when they're not married.' I was shamed, degraded and me, a nice, innocent girl whose parents taught that only bad girls have sex before they marry, I was now a disgrace – a common tart. I was now fodder for town gossip. Oh, my poor mother.

Mack stood up, standing each leg either side of me and then bent over me to pull my light cotton pyjama pants from my ankles to wipe blood from himself. He tossed my pyjama pants back onto my body, then quietly, avoiding passing my parent's bedroom, slipped into the thick blackness of the night. My ankles still bound, sitting on the blanket distressed and confused, I was left to cry and cry hysterically. I did not know what to do. I just sat and cried.

I moved to untangle the sanitary belt from my ankles and I saw the blood. There was blood all over my legs and a new fear grabbed me. I could not let anyone see my blood, and my panic rose to a new height. I had to do something to hide my shame. The galvanised steel water pipes ran along on top of the hot, sandy soil and kept the water supply warm for most of the night. Freed from my belt and napkin and with tears streaming down my face, I traipsed barefooted across the sand to the yard tap and turned the garden hose on.

The hose lay across the lawn. I took hold and let the warm, clean water pour over me from head to toe. I washed and washed my body and my clothes. Then I did it all over again. All the while, I was afraid someone would see me. Any time, Father could come outside to the lavatory. No one must see me. I must not tell anyone, I thought. If my mother should find out I was no longer a good girl, she would be devastated. I could not bring shame to my mother.

A long time passed. I sat scared, crying, shaken and wondering what to do. Secret, yes! Tell no one. Tonight must be my secret, my shame. I had never had secrets from my parents before but now I must.

I crept quietly to my room and cried for the rest of the night.

This was not an act of violent rage and sexual wantonness. It was an act of objective premeditation, an opportunity, cunning and purposeful in its execution. This was an act by a man who knew what he was doing, who well knew the consequences for young girls in a small town. This was an act of control and a means to achieve what he wanted.

And I often wonder how it was he removed the mosquito net and my clothes, why it was that I did not then wake from my sleep.

Years later, I know this was not a case of violent brutal assault or threats to my life, but it had serious consequences for me which catapulted my life into a previously unknown life of secrets, violence and shame.

And still, years later, I cannot find words to describe the moment the realisation entered my consciousness that my life had changed for ever. I was no longer a 'good girl'. There are no words that allow me to explain what this subjugation, this dishonouring action, meant. Nor could I foresee the consequences it would have for me. But what I did know was that this night his presence on top of me heralded humiliation and public disgrace – if anyone found out. I was ashamed and felt I was to blame. What had I said? What had I done that caused him to do what he did to me? In our small town, society said it was always the girl's fault. It was my fault. I should not have slept outdoors at night.

What could I do? Who could I tell? Would I get a baby and how would I know? I could ask no one. I was chaste, not street-smart. I knew nothing about these things. All that I knew was, it was common belief in the 1950s that it was the girl's fault if she had sex before she was married. Even if a girl was raped, it was her fault. She had let him, she had consented. There was no redemption, no deliverance from blame. I was now no longer a pure virgin. I had disgraced my family.

'Don't you bring trouble to this house,' my proud mother had said, 'or you'll go to Vaughan House where all the bad girls get sent.'

*

Time went by and I told no one. I walked around for days in a fuzzy haze. My head was woolly. I was bewildered and tormented by what had happened to me. I felt a strong fear that I would be pregnant and my parents would learn I had disgraced them. For weeks, I lived with fear. I kept the secret. I told no one. I was only sixteen and had my innocence stolen from under the noses of my parents in my own backyard. I had to keep the secret, I had to protect my parents from the shame that their daughter was now 'a bad girl', that l was worthless, 'used goods'.

I did all I could to avoid him, but he hung around, scoffing and reminding me that I was damaged goods. If I sought to avoid him, he would remind me of my predicament and tell me that no self-respecting family would accept me now. I would have no friends. I felt intimidated. My mother, he said, would learn that her daughter was shamed and ruined. Then he kept pressuring me to marry him. Marry! That was ridiculous. I was a child. I knew I was too young, still too young to be a nurse, too young to leave my mother. He was persistent and I found it difficult to avoid him.

During my many years of involvement with domestic violence issues, I was shocked to learn this was a common ordeal for young teenage girls. Some married their assailant to avoid the shame and social stigma. Others made a hasty secret retreat from their home to charity homes for unmarried pregnant girls; their parents sent them away and they became 'unmarried mothers' alone and without family support. They suffered terrible moral reproach.

In time, I bowed to the threats, the pressure, the dishonour, the stigma and the guilt. I surrendered my free will in exchange for my mother's dignity and my personal and family reputation.

A few months later, hostage to my fate, I agreed to become engaged, not married. I accepted engagement because I felt I would soon be old enough to start nursing and then I could escape. But it was not as simple as that.

When I turned eighteen, I married the man who had raped me.

2

1960–1970: Marriage and a Family

My parents never saw through Mack's distortion of character. They never saw what he really was when he was not with them. He was always careful to be polite and helpful when they were around, but my little sister, eleven-year-old Dianne, saw what I saw. She did not like him at all and would call him 'home-wrecker' when he came around.

He would laugh at me in a scornful, smug way. I stalled marriage for as long as I could. He said if I didn't marry him straight away, he would tell my mother that her daughter was ruined. He would spread the message around town and leave me and my family to face the disgrace. He himself could leave town. There would be no consequences for him, and then he would laugh. I was constantly in fear he would tell my mother and he used that threat whenever he wanted to get his own way. Engagement made matters worse. He availed himself of my body. I had no honour to protect now, and anyway, I was now his, he said.

My happy, joyful childhood had come to an end. I had to acknowledge this was not going to go away and I would have to face it. I would have to do what all girls who were not nice girls have to do, and to do it before I got pregnant. Mack was applying heavy, constant pressure to get married and so, finding the situation unbearable – the fear of 'having to get married' – I gave in. But when he told my parents, something had modified their attitude and they would not hear of marriage, said I was too young and refused to give permission. I hated going against them, but I was terribly afraid. And they knew nothing of my fears or my secret.

My family was split apart and, for the first time, was faced with disharmony. In my desperation, I saw that my only course was to persuade them to relent, before I disgraced them in scandal. In my mind, I had to safeguard them from the knowledge and dishonour of their daughter and might become pregnant out of marriage. In my young, naïve mind, an 'honourable' wedding would protect their respectability, as well as my own. Marriage would make respectable that which was not.

Grudgingly, my parents relented. Aunties were contacted for catering and arrangements were made. Mack kept up a public picture and maintained a quixotic courtship. He was charming, charismatic and entertaining for the short weeks leading up to the wedding. He did what he could to appease my parents. My wise sister Dianne continued to despise him. He came to church regularly and we socialised with Jo and Jock at church-held functions, attended church fund-raising fairs and youth sing-songs, and we went to the pictures and picnics as four of us. We also spent hot evening with other family members, aunts, uncles and cousins. Mack was generous with gifts of flowers and books for my mother and attended to Father's boat engine with bits and pieces. He seemed to be always fussing around the boat, cleaning, repairing paintwork and other things to do with Father's boat. Weeks before the marriage date, he purchased a huge second-hand Simpson washing machine, which cost him three weeks' wages. He believed it would emancipate me from the drudgery of hand-washing. He was especially helpful to my parents, and life went on like an everyday family.

Perhaps marriage would not be so bad after all, I thought.

*

We had a normal town wedding with all the usual fuss and bother during a March heatwave. The aunties cooked more cakes and delicacies than could be consumed and the jelly cakes all melted in the extreme heat. I wore my cousin's lace wedding gown and Jo got to be my bridesmaid. Father walked me down the aisle to the altar of our church, while Mother wore her specially acquired, fabulous, mother-of-the-bride outfit. It all seemed deceptively proper.

Even my sad tears hid my secret shame. 'The bride was so happy she cried…' Little did the well-wishers know that I was crying for my loss. I cried for the nurse I would never be and, less than two weeks later, I cried when I found out that he had changed, that he was no longer the man he had pretended to be. Within a week of marriage, his good-natured demeanour disappeared. We had all been duped into taking part in a thespian charade, a planned and deceitful pretence.

I was to quickly learn there was a very dark side to him and now there was no turning back. In the 1950s/60s no one left a 'respectable' marriage. And divorce in my family was unheard of.

*

Our first home was a two-roomed flat in a row of five, in a besser-block building. One week into the marriage an extraordinary event occurred. I will have to tell this in detail because it is important to my whole story.

The fishing season was over and now it was tomato season. Father grew an abundance of them. I was in the kitchen, picking up tomatoes out of hot water and peeling them for lunch with my long-blade fish knife.

Mack was sitting at the table reading a paper when he suddenly looked up and asked, 'What's taking lunch so long?'

I told him I was peeling the tomatoes.

He was furious and shouted impatiently at me, 'Are you stupid? You don't peel tomatoes.'

I continued taking the tomatoes out of the hot water and said with nonchalant confidence, 'My mother peels tomatoes so that's what I do.'

'No one peels fuckin' tomatoes, you stupid cow.'

What? What did he say? No one in my entire family would dare utter such words. I just looked up at him in amazement. I had never heard such language in all my born days. My eyebrows frowned and my squinting face glared at him. I continued peeling the tomatoes.

Suddenly, without warning, he jumped like a Jack-in-the-box, out of his chair, took two steps in my direction and with one swoop of his arm, swiped at the bowl of tomatoes together with the saucepan. Tomatoes went hurling through the air. They hit the wall and splattered. Soft, squashy, red tomatoes all over the floor. More mushy tomatoes dribbled down the wall of our rented flat.

I was dumbfounded. My mouth fell open but I could say nothing. I stood rigid, with the knife limp in my hand.

Unexpectedly, and with instantaneous speed, he grabbed the knife from my grip. I stood frozen in place, totally baffled, my head saying 'Run' but my legs unable to move. Then he let out a barrage of abusive language. On and on it went. I had never heard such a torrent. He came close and held the knife to my throat, his foot standing on my foot so that I couldn't move. I almost fainted. I stopped breathing and stood mute in case I moved a fraction closer to the knife.

Then he began a macabre allegretto dance – pitter, patter, pitter, patter. I was so afraid the knife would pierce my skin. He seemed distracted, as if he did not know what to do next, so I slowly slid my feet backwards until I could no longer feel the knife at my throat. Then I moved even further back towards the loosely ajar screen door, hoping a neighbour would appear. Without really aiming, he threw the knife at me. I moved. It hit the wall, gouging out a small chunk of plaster.

I was exhausted, but filled with an enormous sense of relief. I was not physically hurt or damaged, but I had never been so afraid in my short life. I stifled a tearful cry.

'Stop snivelling. Nothing happened. You're not hurt,' he said. A phrase I was to hear many times in the coming years.

With a twisted, angelic face but no further indication that anything had happened, he sauntered back to his chair and began reading the paper again. Except for my invisible, thumping heart and the sloppy, pulpy mess on the floor and walls, everything was normal again. Although I was dazed and confused, I found my equilibrium and cleaned up the tomatoes from the wall and off the floor. I carried on as though nothing untoward had happened. It was bizarre.

My mother once told me, 'Don't ever let a man hit you,' but she never told me about anything like this.

At the first opportunity, I told my father about Mack's strange outburst.

'Did he hit you?' my father said as he pulled his needle through a hole in a fishing net.

'No,' I said, 'but I was scared at what he would do, and I didn't know what to do.'

My father looked up at me. 'Were you hurt?' he asked.

'No, but I was afraid of what he would do.'

'Well, girl, you weren't hit, you weren't hurt, you made your bed and now you can lie in it.'

I sensed that my father was extremely disappointed in me for marrying against their wishes and his approach was that I would just have to cope with what I had chosen.

*

After a while, I returned to my usual, happy self and was able to put the knife incident behind me. I had no idea why it had happened or what had been the cause or what exactly had happened, but now things seemed okay.

Normal and happy for me was like my parents' home, where we all did things together. Every night after dinner, Mother washed the dishes and my father and sister wiped them. It was my job to put them all away in their correct place. So I thought when I was married it would be normal for my husband to help with the washing up.

'Sure,' he said, when I asked him to dry the dishes.

I was relieved. I thought he might object.

All was going well when 'Oops!' A cup fell from his hand and he threw his arms in the air in an act of innocence.

'Be careful. That was a cup from the set my mother gave me,' I said. I was disappointed.

He went on to plead his innocence and gave me a sly look of blamelessness as he retorted, 'It was your fault. You didn't wash the detergent off.'

He repeated the accident and I became wary, as more of my dinner set smashed into smithereens and disappeared into the bin. After a few more wash-up nights, I knew that if he was to continue to 'help' I would have no dinner set left. I had lost half the crockery gifts my mother had given me through his 'accidents'. I wondered how I would explain it to my mother.

*

It was two months into the marriage when the Reverend came to see me. As he was leaving, Mack arrived home from work in the afternoon. He saw the Reverend walk away from the flat.

'What's that fuckin' sponge doing here?' he sneered.

My mouth fell open with surprise. 'He's come to see me, to see why I haven't been to church.'

On Sundays, I had had no time for myself because Mack always found some place to go, or something to do – barbecue with his friends, meetings with his friends, always his friends.

'Well, I don't want him coming here. He and his kind are just a bunch of parasites.'

I was shocked. No one spoke like that, especially about our Reverend. Mack was saying rude words that I was sure the Reverend could hear and I was deeply embarrassed. After that, I was constantly harangued with derogatory and truculent comments about the Reverend, so much so that in my humiliation, it became easier to abandon going to church. So much for Mack's church attendances before we married! He had led my family and me to believe he would join our family's church but he did the opposite.

Soon, my friend Jo and Jock also stopped coming to see me. Mack insulted them and they began to avoid me.

'They don't like you. They're just jealous,' he would say and add, 'They're stupid, and you don't need them.' Antipathy came easily to Mack and he was eager to tell me about others' faults. He developed a strong aversion to anyone I knew or anyone I talked to.

He also had a loving, caring, protective side as a husband and he fanned his affection with frequent gifts. When we were all warm and cuddly in bed, he would often say in a beguiling way, 'Now you're married, you don't tell other people what goes on in our house. I expect my family to be loyal. Our life is our business and no one else needs to know what we do. It's our secret.'

I knew about secrets. The words 'loyalty' and 'secret' were to become synonymous. Since I was shamed, I had subconsciously been loyal and kept the secret of his abusive behaviour. I was later to call this ongoing behaviour The Families' Secrets Act of 1960. Four months before, my life had so completely changed. My planned future had come to nothing. My relationship and now unfortunate marriage had many hidden elements. I had lost my job, been physically restrained and shamed, subjugated and morally humiliated. I had been threatened with a knife, verbally abused, deceived and lied to. I was cut off from family and friends.

And now in the coming month of December, not yet nineteen years old, I was to be a mother. I called my baby girl Jacqueline (I was impressed by the elegance of American first lady Jacqueline Kennedy). My mother liked the name, but Mac hated it and changed the spelling to Jacquelynne. I was bewildered when Mack was happy and thrilled and cuddled her tenderly. I cried a lot for no reason and Mack in an aggressive mood would demand, 'Why are you crying? What have I done?'

He would thump the table and poke and stab me with his finger. 'Shut up the crying. You're just trying to make me feel guilty.'

I cried more. I had no explanation for my teary outbursts and was fearful about being such a young mother.

When Jacquelynne was only three weeks old, Mack bought an old Bedford utility from his mate with suspect brakes and a dicky starter motor. He decided we would join some of his workmates camping and fishing over the Christmas break on the beach twenty miles down the gulf. I protested because it was late December and the week's temperature was well over the century Fahrenheit. He had decided that a baby would not interfere with his social life, so he insisted we were going.

Within a few hours of arriving at the camp, Jacquelynne was showing signs of heat distress. I wanted to go home but Mack would have none of that. He would not leave the hot camp and take us home. 'Just you look after her. Stop her screaming.'

I became more and more desperate as I saw her deteriorating. The screaming stopped as she was getting lifeless and floppy. When he was distracted with his mates, I wrapped her in a wet towel on the front seat of the Bedford, cranked the engine and raced the car out of the sand dunes right to my mother's house, where I sounded the horn. Mother instinctively knew something was wrong, yanked open the car door, rushed Jacquelynne into the house and immersed her in water in the kitchen sink. All the while she was giving me a good telling off for letting my baby nearly die.

Slowly Jacquelynne recovered and I was glad to spend the rest of the weekend in my own bedroom with Jacquelynne, close to the safety of my own mother.

*

We moved to a new housing estate on the East-side in the first month of 1961. I was glad to be leaving the West-side, because I had less chance of running into our previous landlords, who were the parents of a girl I went to school with. The hole gouged into the plaster wall had increased in size and one of the doors that divided the rooms had holes punched in it on one side. A window was cracked; it happened when he threw his big steel capped boot at me – I was quick to move aside.

Although complaisant by nature, I was also sanguine and hopeful he would change. I noticed that even my mother had become wary, only visiting me when he wasn't home. She never said anything and I was not about to tell her my 'secrets'. At about this time, however, Mother begged Father to purchase a block of land on the West-side close to the beach where I had swum as a child, and a short distance from them. I later wondered if she was worried about me and wanted me close at that time, because Father put the deeds in my name, even though it took all his savings. There was talk in the family of Mack and Father building a small dwelling on the land.

Three years later, Mack persuaded me to transfer the land into his name, and then sold it. Mack bought a small Volkswagen with the money. Father was furious and hardly spoke to me for a long while. I couldn't blame him.

*

Life with Mack was not all bad, but it was unpredictable. At any moment, he could erupt into a mad rage. His behaviour was inconsistent and the only resort open to me was to keep my distance and respond with composure as any flicker of word from me could escalate a volatile event. My course was to wait for the dark cloud to lift and hope. Darkness could last for days, but hope stayed for ever. It was not unusual, after a terror-raising episode, for me to spend days in silence.

Downtime could happen any time, any place, but always in seclusion. A simple night out at the drive-in theatre had the potential to become lethal. Jacquelynne was near newborn and cried a lot. Her carry sleep-basket was on the back seat and I was nursing her in the front seat. She was crying, and nothing would soothe her.

'Shut the kid up,' he said with annoyance.

I did my best to try to stop her crying but was at a loss what to do.

'Keep her quiet!' His patience was running out as she kept crying.

'I want to go home.' My plea to him had no effect. He refused to take us home.

'Just shut her up!'

'I want to go home,' I pleaded again, but I knew we were not going anywhere.

Her crying continued and he got angrier. I got more anxious. Her crying became louder and more distressed. Without saying anything more, he grabbed the bundle out of my arms, twisted towards the back of the car, and flung her violently onto the back seat. I felt her bang up against the backrest and to my horror, she stopped crying. My heart missed many beats and I thought she was dead. She had to be dead. She made no sound. She was so little and the bang against the backrest was so hard. She had to be dead.

I grabbed the door handle to get out of the car and go to her. He snatched at my right arm and held me fixed to the seat. I struggled and tried to open the car door, but he leant across me and locked it. I moved my hand towards the locking knob and he raised his hand, threatening to strike. I retreated into myself and spent the rest of the evening frozen to the seat and crying silently, too afraid to move.

'Stop snivelling. Shut up,' he kept saying to me, but I couldn't.

The film finished and he aggressively rammed the gears of the car into action. We drove the short distance home. I leapt out of the car almost before it came to a stop, grabbed the back door and reached for her. She was alive and sucking her thumb. I fussed over her, wrapping her snug and all was well with us both.

*

Not so long ago, I felt that I had to tell my daughter about this night. With tears in my eyes, I asked her to forgive me for not protecting her when she was a tiny distressed baby.

She put her arms around me and said with a cheeky smile, 'It's all right, Mother dear, I always wondered why I hated the drive-in – and now I know. Don't worry, I won't make you wear odd socks when you're old.'

*

In the 1950s and 1960s, our town was a source of plentiful employment for any men who arrived in the town. They could find jobs in either of our two major industries – the railways or the power station. There was, however, no employment for most young women and there was an unwritten rule that married women were forbidden to work. In those days, financial independence for women was virtually unheard of. Women could not borrow money from a bank without the signature of their husbands, nor could they take out hire purchase, and women could not vote in some government elections.

Mack had introduced me to the Labor Party and I became a member before I was eligible to vote. We were regulars at the monthly branch meetings and participated in all the state and federal election and Labor Party activities. I was the only woman to participate in the monthly meetings. Other wives went to the meetings only to take charge of the suppers.

Workers regularly exchanged employment between the power station and the railways, and Mack joined in. He left his power station construction job to enrol with the safe work instructions course, which would enable him to work with the railways on the rolling goods trains. It paid a working man well. Mack had a photographic memory and was a voracious reader. He could read a book and recite word for word from any page. He was quickly ready to be examined in the railway's safe work practices. It was normally a six-week course but he passed after only three. He joined the railways and moved quickly up the wage scale. That meant regular time away from home, from three to four days at a time.

*

One night, we were on the beach and a youth who was under the supervision of Mack at work walked past us and made a comment of some kind which I did not hear. Mack flew into a rage and the boy ran off. A few days later, Mack caught him walking along the road while he was in his car. He bailed the boy up against the fence with the car. The boy could not run away or move. Mack got out of the car and bashed him mercilessly. The boy's father reported the bashing to the police; Mack was charged with assault but only lightly fined. He pleaded that the boy had used 'insulting' language to his wife and the court believed him.

I had very long hair when I was young and wore it in 1950s/60s fashionable teenage ponytail. On a whim, I decided to have it cut short. Mack was furious and went into a violent arm-waving, foot-stamping rage, first at me and then at the man at the hairdresser's. He left the house storming, screaming he would teach 'the bastard' – the hairdresser – a lesson. I don't know what he did, but I was not welcome back for a second cut.

*

It was during one of his work trips away that a close neighbour came to my door. I didn't know her but called 'Come in' as I saw her approach. She was crying. I made a pot of tea. I was surprised when she told me her story, seeing that she didn't know me. Her husband had collected his full fortnight's pay and had run off with a younger woman. She had no money, no food for her two boys and was going to be evicted from her trust home. She and her boys were destitute.

'You know the local member of parliament, don't you?' she said. 'I saw you handing out how-to-vote cards at the state elections. Would you please ask him if he could help me?'

Of course I would. The next monthly meeting of the Labor Party was too far away, so I went to Mr Riches, our local MP, straight away. He told me to send her to our local welfare officer. I passed this on to her. She attended an interview with the welfare man and after the meeting she came to me and told me that the welfare man had decided she did not qualify for financial assistance.

'That's ridiculous. Of course you would qualify. What about the children? What happened at the interview?'

He had asked her questions, and then said that he would consider her case. When she went back, he said that she did not qualify for any money.

'What did he ask you?' I queried.

I was flabbergasted when she said that he wanted to know what food she cooked for her husband, how often she cooked meat and other silly questions about her cooking and then he asked – here she stammered with humiliation – how often they had sex. I could not believe it. It was shameful to ask such private questions about their life.

'Yes,' she went on, 'I almost fell off my seat, I was so embarrassed. I didn't know where to look.'

When she had returned after the questions, he told her it was her fault her husband had left because she did not give him good enough meals and not enough sex. It was difficult to comprehend what she was telling me.

She left my house with food from my own shopping and then I rallied the neighbours, including my cousins, and we managed to refill her pantry.

Inevitably, one morning, from my kitchen window, I saw a truck pull up outside her house. There were people standing around, one woman police officer, housing trust people and other men, all there to evict her, her children and her belongings. Watching her little boys' toys being loaded into that truck squeezed my heart. I could not hold back the tears. I didn't go to her. I thought that the indignity for her was already overwhelming enough without extra spectators.

Watching my neighbour, from the security of my home, being

evicted, greatly affected me. It pained me to see her standing alone on the pavement, watching strange men hauling her belongings from the house. I sensed her powerlessness, and her position of destitution tormented my sense of justice.

I have never forgotten the image of her and the children and the message I got from her experience: 'Women, abide by your man no matter what, or you too can be faced with poverty, eviction, hungry children and desolation – and don't expect help from welfare or any other agency.'

*

My husband was a good reliable worker and worked long shifts and extra times for additional money. He would chase any job in the railway system that paid more money. I considered myself lucky that my daughter and I were so well provided for. To add to the finances, Mack joined the army reserves when his friend Gary told him they paid members who attended training sessions. They got even more money if they completed week-long camp sessions. Mack and Gary signed up for a ten-day camp.

Gary and his wife, Iris, had two boys one younger and one the same age as my first-born daughter. They were the only couple we met socially at their house. No one was ever invited to ours. Later, Gary joined the army full-time and while he was interstate completing his preparations to be included in the first Australian deployment to Vietnam, I visited Iris occasionally and got to know her better as time went on. As she was the wife of his friend, my husband could hardly object.

Iris and I were both pregnant the same time. She had another boy and I had my second daughter, born late into the second year of my marriage in 1962.

*

Mack was a complex person, an enigma who read Shakespeare aloud to me from his book The Complete Works of Shakespeare, and he read love poems to me from C.J. Dennis, his favourite being 'Er name's Doreen'. He said it was equal to any of Shakespeare's sonnets. He would give a pause and wink at me and say Annette instead of Doreen. When my daughter was still very young, Mac would read poems to her from Banjo Paterson, his favourite being 'A Bush Christening'. He himself read George Orwell, D.H. Lawrence, Steinbeck and other classics of the time. He bought records of classical music and many of them were familiar to me from my mother's collection.

Mack was a very intelligent man. I know this, because he often told me so.

Our bookcase also swelled with books by Marx, Lenin and other similar left-wing writers. Under his tutoring, I was well instructed on socialism and became a follower of social reform. When I remembered my evicted neighbour, I developed a particular interest in women's social reforms. I began to see how women were restricted in matters of finance, education and employment and housing, and I thought that the drudge of housework was soul-destroying. There was something that had always concerned me when I was fourteen and working in the grocery store. I had to lift and lug 70-pound bags of sugar onto benches to be weighed into six-, four- and two-pound bags. It was not the weight or work that I minded, but I was paid less than the boys working in the section of the emporium merely selling tools.

'That's because boys have to pay for your ticket to the pictures,' was the manager's explanation and the regular dictum of the day.

The 'inequality of women' in society had not been inscribed into language in those days.

*

Mack's behaviour up to now had been all loquacious rants, raving threats and rancorous outbursts. Over time, I had learned to cope with his vainglorious boasting behaviour even though I always felt embarrassed by his ever-expanding profanities and was often excruciatingly upset. I seemed to always be crying. Sometimes I would say whatever he was complaining about had been my fault, just to shut him up, but that didn't work. I confessed to one object, he moved to a different scenario and the harangue continued. Mostly I would switch off my hearing aid, to cut down on much of the blustering volume of his voice. I was not profoundly deaf, so the haranguing noise got through and, of course, there was no mistaking the taut, angry face and physical expression of rage. He would erupt with a rapid tempo of intimidating words. It had been my schooldays experience to switch off attention to what was happening when I could no longer follow what was taking place. So I retreated into my own world when things became difficult for me.

*

Until my second daughter was born I had not experienced serious physical violence (apart from the knife at my throat), just violent pushing, shoving, finger poking, raised clenched fists, occasional bruises and the racing rants of a verbal onslaught, but things were about to change dramatically.

Mack was standing in the doorway with his fist in a ball. I walked past him and, to my amazement, without a word he punched me in the back. I lunged forward, bumping into the door. I was dazed and he quickly punched me again and again until we were in the bedroom. He roared like an animal thrashing about. He flung his outstretched arm across my dressing table and swiped all my crystal settings Mother had given to me onto the floor. Everything broke and the only surviving piece left was the crystal tray – it lives with me today with a big chip out of one side.

He pulled clothes from my robe and ripped garments to pieces. His strength was enormous and he flung me onto the bed, shut the door and began pulling my clothes off and ripped them apart. He thrashed me with my bra; the hooks drew blood. My hearing aid tumbled around the bed and I was afraid it would be damaged and I would be without it. He ripped my clothes to pieces then he pulled his belt from his trousers and I felt immediate terror as he swung it threateningly and then thrashed me with the buckle, pounding my flesh. I drew my legs to my chin. Blood ran down my legs and I rolled into a ball. He grabbed and pulled me apart…

A few months later, when he physically attacked me again, the violence of the attacks was increasing. And so were his presents for my two daughters and me. I wondered if it was his way to say sorry? Whatever! I was not swayed.

*

In summer, it was always a challenge to stay cool in this arid land and in the summer of 1963–1964 there was a particularly long drawn-out heatwave. For days at a time, temperatures reached 117°F (50°C) in our house. I maintained a minute-by-minute, twenty-four-hour vigil to keep the babies safe. The bathtub was filled with water, I constantly ducked the girls in and out and I turned on the shower and let water drizzle over them at intervals during the long day. For myself, I just stepped in and out from under the shower, shorts, shirt and all. Yes, I dripped water around the house, but the house came a long way down the list for consideration when it came to be surviving such heat. Clothes and our bodies dried rapidly on those days.

When the girls became sleepy and wanted their afternoon nap, I covered them with wet sheets while they lay in their beds. I turned a gentle electric fan on while they slept. It mattered not that their bed got soaked; sheets dried in moments anyway. I would regularly lift the covers and fan them before replacing wet sheets as soon as they dried. Babies have died in such conditions and many young mothers did not know how to look after their babies in extreme weather. During my days of helping out at the hospital, lots of older people and babies were admitted for their safety. The hospital had large ceiling fans, which helped a little.

That day, a cool change from a west wind came in late in the afternoon but the house was still hot.

Mack could contain himself no longer. All day, his distress had been rising. His temper slowly came to the boil. 'It's your fault the house is so fucking hot! You left the fucking blinds up!' He was pacing the passage as the verbals kept coming.

I was too occupied with the care of my daughters to pay much attention. As I stepped out of their room into the narrow passage, I accidentally bumped into him. Without warning, he grabbed me around the throat with both hands, immediately cutting off my breath. With incredible strength, he lifted me off the floor, my feet kicking and dangling. He was choking me. He grabbed me by the neck and shook me like a wet rag, then pinned me up against the wall. I could not breathe. My feet hung loose and I felt myself fading. I knew I had only three minutes without oxygen to live as I slid down the wall into unconsciousness on the floor of the passage.

I have no idea how long I was blacked out. Consciousness slowly oozed to my awareness of lying horizontal on the floor. I stayed lying motionless trying to gather my thoughts wondering, where am I? Am I dead? Then I felt jabs in my back and knew I was not dead. He was gently kicking – prodding me with his boot. I moved slightly and groaned and the gentle nudging stopped. He could see I was alive and he walked away. Without moving a finger or a hair, I opened my blurry eyes, looked around and saw I was in the kitchen by the back door. How did I get there? I felt an alarm bell go off in my head. My throat hurt when I swallowed and I thought, 'He's trying to kill me.' Was he dragging me out the house? Was he trying to dispose of my body? I thought I was going to die if I stayed in the house. I had to get out.

Survival mode switched on and I sprang to my feet afraid for my life and took off faster than a gazelle. I was running for my life, out the back door, down the steps, across the sandy backyard, bare-footed over three-corner jacks, across the road, over the neighbour's low fence, intending to bang on their door. Fear, real life-threatened fear is anaesthetic: when you run, you run for your life – nothing else matters, staying alive is all you feel. I felt no pain nor the three-corner jacks in my feet.

*

He was close on my heels.

I was a school champion runner and ran very fast but failed the fence jump and landed face-down into horse poo among the flowing rose bushes and he too had vaulted the fence and was right there, towering over me, hands on hip panting for breath. I tried to bury my body under the rose bushes but to no avail.

'Get up!' he yelled. 'Fuckin' get up!'

I did not move. I froze, praying that a delay and his yelling might rouse the neighbour to come and rescue me, but nobody came. People did not get involved in 'family quarrels'.

'Get up,' he kicked me hard in the ribs. 'Get up.'

I did not move. He kicked me some more, but I refused to move and he kicked several more times. Then he picked me up like a sack of wheat, threw me back over the fence and dumped me on the footpath. I crumpled onto the ground. He jumped over to my side of the fence and kicked me again. I did not move. I could not move. Terrified to go back in the house, I feared for my life, but I was helpless. I could run no more.

He grabbed me by the hair and pulled me to my feet. I was faint with fear. I struggled to stand and sank down onto the gravel footpath again. He kicked me and pulled me up. I still refused to move. I feared if I were to return to the house, I would die. He thumped his fist into my back. I stepped forward to prevent myself from tumbling over and he thumped me again to make me take another step. He kept this up, a knuckle punch into my back – one step forward, repeated all the way back across the road and into our backyard, where he dragged me into our house.

Inside, he left me and attended to his preparation for his four-day train duty.

I staggered in to see my babies were asleep and noticed the horse poo stuck to my wet clothes. I went to the bathroom, stood under the shower, dropped my clothes into the bath and, wrapped in a towel, swayed with a limp onto my bed. I had been numbed until then, but now I felt the excruciating stabs of pain. My ribs ached sharply when I took breath and I felt them, knowing there were at least two broken or at least cracked. I would be black and blue tomorrow and then the real pain would come. (Chest X-rays many years later show evidence of cracked or broken ribs from history.)

He came in to the room to tell me he would take the car to work. I said nothing to him. I was in too much pain to speak. But in my head, I was saying, 'Go to hell!'

The pain in my chest made it difficult to breathe and after he had gone, with my arms wrapped around my chest, I dragged myself to the linen storage cupboard. There I found two old, worn flannel napkins. I made triangular bandages and, with my one arm and my teeth holding the bandage edge, tied my ribcage together with knots on the least painful side. With one mobile arm, I made my babies' night-time bottles, settled them for the night and took myself off to lie on the bed. I managed to secure my arm to my chest, which had also been at the end of a steel-capped boot kick, propped my body up with pillows, leaning my most injured side against the pillows, leaving my less injured side to do the breathing with the least pain, and tried to settle.

Next day, I could not move. I was indeed a mess of bruising all over. I waited until the girls cried for attention. All I could do for them was get food and warm milk and feed them in their cots. I had no strength to lift them out. They were good babies. My eldest, who would have toddled around on the floor, made no complaint at being confined to her cot. She remained there while I one-handedly changed her nappy and fed her for three days between me lying on my bed recovering. Somehow, we managed to get through the days together.

Mack arrived home and saw my distress. He said nothing. I said nothing.

*

In Port Augusta, in the late 1950s, it was common knowledge that Mr McKenzie mercilessly belted Mrs McKenzie. Mr McKenzie was a huge, tough, bear of a man and Mrs McKenzie was a tiny, fragile butterfly. Her distorted face carried the hallmarks of a broken nose, broken cheek- and jawbones, and a broken eye socket. Her face was a permanently distorted mess of scarring and odd shapes. She walked the streets of town, her face bent downward, but nothing could hide her felt shame. I often wondered why Mr McKenzie was not ever charged with assault when the evidence was so clear. It told me that husbands were allowed to bash their wives.

Most times, Mrs McKenzie would be admitted to the hospital, where she was secreted off to a private room, but one time Dr Coats put her in the main women's ward in the middle bed. It was rumoured that Dr Coats had been a champion boxer in his younger days and, on that day, he belted Mr McKenzie to a pulp and made him sit by his wife's bed, surrounded by all the other women. The good doctor made him take care of his wife, fetch her bedpans, help her eat food, bring her water.

I witnessed all this because my mother was a regular inpatient at the hospital, sometimes spending several weeks at a time recovering from chronic asthma. I had caught the bus to the hospital every night to visit and that night my mother nodded her head for me to look across the ward. I saw Mr McKenzie with black eyes and his face all puffy. I saw Mrs McKenzie, her face a full purple and blue, like a dying autumn moon, slipping down between the white sheets. She looked like death.

'Never let a man hit you!' my mother said to me.

And now, three years after my mother's advice, I was lying three days in my own bed with my painful body and damaged ribs. I knew what she had intended me to hear, but she never did tell me how I could prevent it.

*

After that near-death experience, the horrible suffocation and bashing, I learnt to read the signs. I was always on guard and learnt to run from the house before he could find a chance to bash me again. I read the warnings of a coming storm. At the first signs, I would check the girls were safe in their room, most of the physical assaults happened at night. They would lie quietly in their beds sucking thumbs and cuddling their teddy bears while his fist splintered the bedroom door and I would be out of the house walking the streets in fear, hiding and sleeping the night in other people's backyards, where I felt safe.

*

Several months after my horror beating, when Mack was due to arrive home later in the morning on the Trans-Australian from Kalgoorlie, I woke to find my sixteen-year-old sister, Dianne, standing over my bed.

'Annette! Annette!' I heard her call as she shook me from my sleep. 'Come quick, Mother has died.' She was crying. Her words did not register and I thought she just needed my help.

'It's all right. I'll come and give her an injection and everything will be all right.'

I had been helping my mother manage her asthma attacks since I was twelve years old. My ability to give my mother injections delivered relief more quickly than waiting for an ambulance or doctor to arrive. Injections of adrenalin were the treatment of the day and when she was suddenly too sick to manage the injecting herself, I took over. Her syringe was kept in a jar of methylated spirits and had to be washed in sterile water before it could be used. Sometimes her asthma attack had advanced too far and she was incapable of carrying out the procedure herself. She was hospitalised frequently. Adrenalin was a potent drug and I was always afraid of it and careful in its administration. It had to be done slowly One millilitre injected per minute so, with the needle still in her arm, five millilitres could take five minutes to deliver. The drug made her heart thump and race madly but it usually quelled the asthma attack. The ambulance was called for and she spent weeks in hospital care.

When my sister was telling me our mother was dead, I did not take it in. I was expecting my mother was simply in a bad way and I could get to her quickly and everything would be all right.

I woke my daughters and without changing their nappies or night clothes, I took them in to my next-door neighbour, a good woman with her own two girls, and she promised to mind mine. Dianne and I rushed to Father's house.

It was true. Mother had passed away. Dianne had sat on the bed beside her, and watched Mother die from an asthma attack as Father ran to the phone box to call the doctor. He was too late. When the doctor arrived, he pronounced her dead and he left. Mother was still in her bed when my sister and I arrived. I could not bring myself to see her as she lay dead. Dianne and I went into shock. My youngest sister was just six years old and had no idea what it would mean for her future. It was a terrible time for us all.

*

After the death of my mother, I contemplated leaving my marriage but the obstacles were enormous. There was no work available. No married women need apply: it was frowned upon for married, separated or divorced women to want to take away the jobs from single girls.

I did find a job for two days while Mack was away, a job that no 'nice' girl would think of doing – a waitress in a hotel. Well, my mother was deceased, and I was no longer a 'nice' girl, and if I was going to leave Mack, I would need work to support my daughters. My mother would have rolled over in her grave if she had ever found out. I worked for two days but the woman looking after my girls told me she couldn't continue. So much for my plans! I realised that even if I were to find work, there would be no one to care for my little girls and no housing for me without a husband, and I would not consider living off my hard-working father. The list of difficulties was insurmountable. I would simply be changing humiliation for poverty, and what would become of my daughters?

There was also my six-year-old sister, who was now without a mother. She was constantly on my mind and I felt she needed me. Not that I could be of much help to her. My shambolic life of fear and constant agitation continued, getting increasingly intolerable, not to mention dangerous. I was alone, without friends or family support, and the pantomime of keeping up the appearance of a wholesome marriage was becoming a struggle. But I kept the family secret and, on the outside, I maintained a complaisant face, professed to have a happy family and carried on.

The politics of the day was an exciting place for me to be and as I grew more comfortable in that circle. I was consumed by it. At the state Labor Party convention in Adelaide, at the new Trades Hall in the mid-1960s, I saw politics at work. There, Clyde Cameron, federal member for Hindmarsh, astounded many delegates when he announced how gracious the Premier Frank Walsh was by planning to step aside to allow Don Dunstan, the new member for Norwood, sufficient time to contest the next election as leader. Frank's face turned white, as he was taken by surprise. The move was breathtaking in its audacity and so began great political and social changes for South Australia as Don Dunstan became premier at the next election.

The Labor Party was blessed with several greats during the 1960s/70s. Gough Whitlam was one of them. He toured my electorate of Grey during the early 1960s federal election campaign. At that time, the electorate of Grey encompassed a huge section of the north of

South Australia and took in major working-class towns. During the campaign tour, he was scheduled to address the obligatory railway workshop knock-off-time-at-the-factory-gate meeting for the workers. All blokes of course!

There had never been a political meeting especially for the women. No one thought to give women a chance to meet our hopefully next prime minister. So, knowing there were only hours to spare between Gough's engagements, I swung into gear to organise a women's 'meet Gough Whitlam'. I contacted Gough's campaign managers and diverted Gough from his 'rest period' to meet women in our town. Our community hall was available, so I spread the word quickly via schools, local radio and bingo meetings and, just to make sure women would turn up, organised to have a fashion parade of expensive jewellery from our local jewellers. The store manager arranged the security. I need not have worried. Women turned up in their hundreds and Gough loved the female attention. Afternoon tea enabled women to have close contact and an opportunity to talk with our prospective next prime minister. Alas, the attention did not win us a Labor government. We had to wait for the next election for that.

In my haste to organise a political rally for women in record time, I forgot to tell the local federal member and other party state officials that I was arranging a women's afternoon, scheduled for four hours before the factory-gate meeting. It was a huge political indiscretion and they were not happy with me. Pfff…they were only blokes, who never gave any thought to us women. But the weekly Australian newspaper reported the women's rally as a Labor Party campaign coup for the electorate.

*

Such confidence politically did not, however, translate to my domestic situation. Politically I was triumphant but domestically I was a meek shadow, hiding my growing secret. In the society of our town, it was a big shame to have married a 'bad' man, and especially bad to have married a violent man. It reflected badly on a wife. She had made the bad mistake; she was the one in the wrong. I struggled to keep my head up, but there came a time when I was forced to be humble and drop all pride for the sake of my life.

I had no one to confide in when things got bad, except for one friend, another 'bad' girl who had rushed into what her family thought was an 'unsavoury' marriage. Fortune favoured her because her choice had been good, her husband a good man, and she bloomed with a joyful family. She was Iris, whose husband Gary had been a workmate of Mack. He was in the army and serving in Vietnam. Iris had two small boys and I had known her since we were school age. We were not close but had reconnected via our husbands. She was rough and tough and came from a coarse family. My mother would have called her 'common'. I developed a different view.

Late one night, I stood at her front door, forsaken and forlorn, no shoes and in disarray. I do not remember the particular incident that caused me to be standing there at midnight. The front light came on. She just looked at me in surprise, saw the tears in my eyes, stretched out her arms towards me and drew me to her tiny little frame. With motherly tenderness, she pulled me inside. She made me a pot of tea and I told her my sad secrets.

She knew. I had no need to explain. I do not know how she knew, but she knew. Then the story of her own sad mother came out later – she was no stranger to a bad marriage

'Leave the bastard, Annette. He's no good,' she said to me.

We talked for hours and she was wise and willing to listen to it all. She had the right empathy and I felt greatly comforted. She made me a bed in the spare room and soon I was settled, even though still upset and exhausted. My body hurt all over. I must have been thrown around the room, but I had no visible signs just then.

Next morning, I was black and blue all over. I wandered down the passage and found Iris in the bathroom cutting her very short, bright orange hair. I hadn't noticed it the night before.

'I always cut my hair when it gets to a hundred,' she said, meaning the temperature of the day.

It was going to be another hot one and I was sure that if the weather continued, she would have no hair left to cut.

'I think I might have overdone the bleach,' she said as she noticed my surprise at her strange orange colour. She was a tiny woman with an olive complexion and that day she looked like an upside-down carrot. She was wearing a green shirt and green shorts with her spiky, bristly, and short, bright orange hair. Punk rockers would love her sense of style!

Pained as I was, I could manage a small laugh – she was a very funny woman and didn't give a damn.

As we ate breakfast, she advised me again to leave the bastard, that he wasn't any good. She attended to her boys and then we continued talking. It was late afternoon, still sunlight, when Mack came to the back door. She had her main door open, with the fly screen locked.

'Yes, she's here,' I heard Iris say. 'No, you can't talk to her. No, she's not going home.'

I heard him say, 'You tell her, if she doesn't come home, she'll never see the girls ever again. They're mine not hers and she'll never have them.'

My heart took a gigantic leap. Oh no! Not the children.

'Oh, piss off! And grow up!' Iris said in disgust.

He left but not without adding more warnings as he departed.

Iris was a brash girl but I loved her attitude and wished I could be like her. She took no shit from anyone. It was inspirational for me to see this tiny woman stand up to the dark force that I was married to.

'Leave him, Annette,' she repeated and then added, 'You can come and live here with me and the kids.'

I cried. No one had ever been so supportive of me in that way before. I was concerned about my children and knew I could never leave them. He had always told me they were not my daughters, they were his. But I was not so sure that he would not harm them – I never knew what he might do.

Later that evening, Mack was again at the back door. This time he had worked out his strategy. I could hear that he had the girls with him and I heard him tell Jacquelynne to tell me to come home. I heard her crying. I was in emotional agony but I did not move off my chair. I clung to the seat with both hands, afraid I would run to the door to embrace and reassure her that I loved them both.

'No, no,' I heard the words in my head. 'I can't go on living like this, afraid all the time.'

'Tell Mummy to come home!'

I heard her pleading, 'Mummy, Mummy, please, please, come home.'

Tears rolled down my face.

'Please, Mummy, please. Please come home, Mummy.'

*

In the mid-1960s the contraceptive pill came to Port Augusta. Many women flocked to their doctor to get prescriptions, and I was one of them.

'No, you don't need the pill. You're young and healthy you can have a baby every year for the next ten years,' the doctor said.

Ten babies! I thought not. I left the surgery in horror and empty-handed.

I became pregnant for the third time and was close to three months pregnant but I did not tell Mack, and a few mornings after another long night of a steel-capped boot kicking, I began bleeding and was in pain.

I usually drove the car to pick him up for lunch, but as I was early I drove a couple of streets on to my auntie's house to ask her what I should do. Of course, I did not mention the kicking! She said I should go to the hospital straight away. I would go in the afternoon. I was late back for him and he was furious. He pushed me out of the driver's' seat across to the passenger side of the car. I quivered in fear as I huddled into the corner.

I got his lunch and he said he would take the car back to work.

'I want the car today.' I said.

'No, I'm taking it back with me.'

Oh no! Now I would have to tell him why I needed the car. He would be angry.

I told him, and he was indeed, very angry.

'You only did this to make me feel guilty,' he said, and his pugnacious diatribe started. He shoved me outside the house and prodded me all the way to the car.

I was admitted to hospital and miscarried next morning.

*

My son was born the next year, in 1966.

Just after the birth, the nurse came to my bed and said, 'My dear, why are you crying? Did you have another baby girl?'

'No. I have two sisters and two daughters and now I have a boy. I'm so happy.'

*

In 1967, I had surgery to give me full hearing in one ear.

An elderly gentleman had approached me and told me that I should not be relying on a hearing aid, that I was too young, and he gave me the name of a surgeon who had successfully restored his wife's hearing. I wrote to the surgeon and he told me to get a referral from my doctor. My doctor said I didn't need the operation, that I was doing all right with the hearing aid. When I wrote back to the Adelaide surgeon, he said I should come and see him anyway.

After a few tests, the specialist announced that I could benefit from the operation, but he could offer no guarantees, no success stories from previous operations. The fact was, he had just returned from London, where he had learnt about the operation and he had only performed one such operation here before. I would be his second. I decided I would do it. I sorted out my cousins to take care of the children and took the train to Adelaide.

I woke from the operation in the recovery room with a whopper of a headache. The surgery had been a 'jackhammer' attack on the diseased middle-ear bone and left me severely concussed. The bone was replaced with a metal prosthesis. I was expecting to wake up and declare, 'I can hear! I can hear!' just like in a Hollywood movie. But no, I could not hear them. I replied to the surgeon's questions with, 'No, I can't hear you. No, I can't hear what you are saying.'

The surgical team gathered around me. They were laughing. 'Yes, Annette. You can hear us.'

'No, no, I can't,' and everyone laughed again.

It turned out I could hear very well, but my brain couldn't accept the change. It was weird. Go to sleep deaf, wake up hearing. My brain took some time to catch up. I returned home and my recovery was long and difficult. My balance had been disrupted and I had a hard time with motion. Walking was a stumble and post-operative advice was to take care not to fall and avoid strenuous activity.

The process had been a success and I no longer needed a hearing aid; or should I say, I managed without one. After the operation, I became very cautious. I was always afraid that Mack might push me violently to the floor as was so often his signature move. The shove and kick to the floor would damage my inner ear, disturb the implanted prosthesis, ending my new-found audio capability. I could hardly ask anyone, 'If my husband assaults me, would that disturb my inner ear?' I was hyper-alert and kept my distance from him. I could put up with verbal abuse.

However, it was not long before he started his push and shove again. When I fell to the floor, I instinctively rolled myself into a ball with my arms around my ears and pleaded with him not to touch my ears. He looked at me, stunned. I had never pleaded before. He just walked away.

*

As a railway worker, my husband was a member of the Australian Workers' Union (AWU) and he was a state delegate to the local United Trades and Labor Party annual conferences. I went with him to all the Labor party conferences in those days. Mack was a staunch partisan, often spouting a belief in egalitarianism. A devotee of unions, he consequently spent time in the AWU local branch office where Jack Wright was the union organiser. Jack was later to become deputy premier of South Australia in the 1970s. Mack was highly competent in matters of industrial law and kept his own records of updates to industrial legislative changes as they came into force. He would talk about them and I found the process of government and legislation interesting.

From my involvement with the Labor Party, I learnt a lot about the power of legislation – more importantly, the power of knowledge and knowing the rules of the party. I learnt that it was important to know the rules and laws of anything that was of interest at the time. All institutions have rules.

It was a time when the state AWU was under strong attack from the ruling federal branch. The federal secretary pulled out all stops and finally sacked all the officials in the SA branch. Their sacking was fervently contested in the Federal Court and the South Australian officials were represented in court by Roma Mitchell. Their defence was strong and at the end of several weeks of court hearings, the SA officials won their case and were all reinstated. After the case, Don Dunstan acknowledged Roma Mitchell's brilliance and she became a QC then a High Court judge. Later, she was appointed Governor of South Australia as Dame Roma Mitchell.

Jack Wright, a friend and close neighbour, took over as state secretary and moved to Adelaide. Mack was appointed as an organiser and was told he had to base himself in another town. We all moved to Port Pirie.

*

Mack borrowed a mate's ute and loaded our furniture and possessions up and made two or three trips to Port Pirie. On the final load was our kitchen equipment and he had organised a work friend to help move the fridge. The two little girls gathered to watch. They clung to my legs and hid their faces, peeping out, then quickly covered their faces again. The fridge moved away from the wall and, lo and behold, three or four leather trouser belts fell to the floor. Mack looked in amazement at the trouser belts lying on the floor, his face twisted in anger, and I stood tense and held the girls close, but he could hardly act out with his mate watching on. The children hid under my dress and gave nervous giggles and I was amused at their cunning. Then my mind quickly turned to horror – what had he been doing with the leather belts that the children should hide them?

*

I was embarrassed by the state of the house we left. There were fist holes through the lightweight hollow drum door. That evidence flew against the declaration he once made to me: 'Never fight with your fists. You have to earn a living with your hands.' As a result, his strong work boots were a constant weapon, and responsible for all the lower-level door damage.

He was streetwise and hence he never, or rarely ever, punched or belted me with his hands. Instead he would headbutt me with skull-busting blows and mind-stunning force that could almost knock me unconscious. Force that threw me off my feet, where I fell to the floor, or a push or a shove, then it was a boot kicking to covered parts of the body. Other times he would push my face into the door – bruising and cut brows were easy to explain: 'She bumped into the door' or 'She fell against the wall.' His hand would grab my hair and drag me around the floor, swinging me into furniture or objects, or smash my face or head into the wall. His signature was to force me to the floor. I would get up and he would push me down again. The more I got up, the more I was damaged. I learnt to just stay on the floor. I never cried during a bashing. I did not want the children to hear my distress and, if I could get away, I would run from the house. I ran for my life and only when I was safe and out of sight did the tears come.

*

Approaching ten years of marriage in Port Pirie, the two girls were in primary school and his violence continued to escalate. A shove, a push, flurried abuse. I managed the situation by shutting down my emotions during his tirades and by escaping and hiding outdoors if I felt trouble was brewing, before I got injured. The children grew up never knowing if their mother would be at home when they woke each morning. They were told over and over that their mother was stupid, she was a liar, not clever and was not brilliant like him, and that they were brilliant because they were of his genes. I was not of his genes, therefore I was stupid. He told them whenever their mother fled the violence leaving the house, that she had left them! He would never leave them and he loved them more than their mother did.

The mantra to me became, 'They're not your children, they're mine, get it!' and the 'Get it?' became more and more strident as time rolled on. Yes, I did get it. I had no rights to the children, and I was becoming invisible and valueless to them.

Bringing back memories of being chased from the house, I wonder if it was his intention for me to vacate, leaving him alone in the house with the children.

His truculence was not exclusive to me. The children were also in line for abuse. In her first school years, my eldest took to reading with gusto and she was always looking to her father to coach her. He regularly told her how smart she was. She often got out her reading books and read aloud to him.

One day she seemed reluctant. She had been avoiding reading to him. He told her to get her book and read what she had learnt that day. We were sitting at the table and he had his back slightly turned away from me. He was listening to her reading and I did not notice at first that he had his foot clamped down on her foot. But I did notice that she had her head bent away from him. I got up from my chair and went to stand beside her. I saw the grimace on her face and realised something was not right. He was squeezing her earlobe and had his thumbnail dug into the soft tissue of her ear. She had tears of pain in her eyes but she defiantly would not cry. I pulled her away from him. She was six years old!

Another time I saw the cruelty was when he was checking that the children had cleaned their teeth. I walked into the room and he again had his foot on her foot. He held her head back too far, and her mouth was forced wide open. His finger was scraping her teeth and gums. His nails were not clean and he scraped so hard that her gums bled. I again pushed him away and pulled her to me. She had bleeding gums and was crying.

My eldest daughter Jacquelynne got the brunt of his aggressive attention. She always yelled at him to leave me alone and would defend me when she could. She was very brave but I remember very little about the younger children. They always seemed to slink away out of sight. It begs the question, how many times did the children suffer in these ways when I did not see and did not know? He was sly and devious in executing pain on the children. His actions were always subtle and rarely obvious. I only learnt in later years that there was more, much more, going on than I ever knew about at the time.

It is my subsequent experiences that have shown me that this cruel torture of children is part of the subtleties of violence carried out under the guise of parenting. Domestic violence includes a spectrum of inappropriate parenting. The two examples I have given are only a glimpse of the cruelty children can be subjected to. It is not possible for the non-violent parent to watch out for the child every moment of the child's life, but we now know it is possible to know that, if there is domestic violence in the home, it goes hand in hand with pain and cruelty towards the children. They also are victims. Appropriate domestic violence legislation will provide protection against undeclared and unseen child abuse.

*

In the late 1960s, Mack quit his employment as an organiser with the AWU and began a job as part of the railway staff with the Hamersley iron mining company in the Pilbara.

Going to the Western Australian Pilbara region was to be an adventure, especially for the children. I hoped my life would be better and that it would be a new start for us all. We sold our possessions and packed up our personal stuff. With a fully loaded Falcon station wagon, Mack drove across the Nullarbor. The first three hundred miles were treacherous, unsealed bulldust sands, and it was not considered a safe journey: getting bogged down in bulldust could leave a family stranded for days at a time. Few adventurers dared the journey. Pulling the small trailer complete with our camping equipment, several gallons of water in two drums and four jerrycans of petrol, we were self-sufficient for our journey. We were to be our own Leyland Brothers adventurers. We were a foolhardy family led by a foolhardy man.

*

A little over a week later, we arrived in Dampier, the central business district and the main port for shipping out the mined iron ore. As the mining had expanded, so had the township, and a new settlement called Karratha was established twenty miles north. It was not many years before early arrivals camped on the beach, but we were settled in large, modern, brand-new houses.

The surrounding landscape was strong, with bold, rugged theatres of jagged ranges and huge canvases of red and purple mosaics of massive expanses of land and rocks. A full gallery of ancient Aboriginal art was to be found everywhere and the roar of the Indian Ocean could be heard in the gentle cool of the evening. It was a very beautiful, strong country which became fragile when disturbed.

The new town continued to grow as many families arrived, day after day. The place was a beehive of housebuilding frenzy. It was easy to recognise the 'locals' as the thick, red dust blew around and settled itself on our clothing and turned our faces a rusty red. However, all they were building were houses, hundreds of houses, and one modern school, and nothing else.

Karratha was a mining town and a mining town meant a men's town. No one considered the needs of the women and children who were to live there. We mothers were promised a kindergarten for our preschoolers, but there was none. Many other promises failed to materialise. There were great plans for Karratha to be a major city, in fifteen to twenty years' time but we were here now and with nothing, nothing but carpets of gibber stones and new houses. Everything was twenty miles away in Dampier. The only doctor in the whole area was also twenty miles away and he was an expert in industrial accidents. He had no family medical experience and was rough and gruff with the women.

*

In this foreign environment, I found I was in the same high and dry situation that I had become used to – a grounded boat with other women and children on board, no water to float us, no paddle to row with, no wind or sail to steer us through this over-rated, under-provided and uncivilised would-be satellite city. Stranded, isolated, with no family or familiar friends, we were common strangers in a sparse, stinking hot, humid, exotic place. We were prisoners of our remoteness and of the exhausting climate, locked inside our perfect, air-conditioned homes with no opportunities to make friends or socialise. The company employment recruiters had promised our families fully functioning facilities. They did not deliver.

I was not happy. For me, the move was a huge disappointment and I was now faced with a new and deeper isolation. However, I was no longer a frightened, intimidated teenager with no friends or no family around me. I was a grown-up, a mother with children, struggling to hold a family together. I was determined to fit in. I had to deal with what this new land dealt me.

My solution was to brave the heat for one hour and venture out of the house each day, knock on doors and invite women to my house for tea and scones. Many came, for they were all feeling like me. Shyness sank as friendships were forged. I catalogued what skills we had between us. I found schoolteachers, early childcare workers, dental nurses, a trained hospital nurse, a librarian and a pharmacist. All the women were excited, willing and anxious to move forward and support our community. We had a new full moon, a guiding light with full vision, and scope for creating an interim women's network. We settled on a loose committee that I was to lead and we women would campaign for what we needed. Together we made up a willing, militant force for the company to reckon with, a strong united front.

We decided that we wanted one of the mining company's four-bedroomed houses for our operations centre. From there we could organise all the other necessary services we might need. I led a deputation to the housing manager; he pleaded no such authority. We bypassed him and headed for the mining company's chief. The company, he said, was not willing to give us what we wanted. It certainly was not a case of 'ask and ye shall receive'. It was not even for the begging. We rallied our forces and tried again, but still management refused us a house.

After an appropriate time lapse for them to have heard us and made suitable responses, which they didn't, I pulled out the big guns. A small deputation of women gave our appointed 'complaints officer' something to ponder over. I suggested that if the company did not give us a women's house, rent-free of course, we women would return to the states we had come from and no doubt (with my fingers crossed behind my back) the men, their newly acquired workforce, would follow us. The officer looked shocked and was speechless. We left him gasping like a fish out of water and told him we would give him a week to think about it.

And just to add flavour to the curry, I called a meeting of all the women in the Karratha township, to meet at the phone box on the corner roadway of the town entrance. Someone must have been worried because the only town police officer drove from Dampier to attend, to be an observer. That 'someone' had the sense to be worried, because hundreds of women braved the heat to voice their displeasure at our being ignored and at being so isolated without the promised services.

We women needed to do no more than show strength in numbers.

*

Our brand-new Women's House was a fabulous success. We moved quickly to establish a play school for our preschoolers. There were no fences around the house, so the building contractors all rallied and put up a fence to keep the children safe. They also established outdoor play equipment. Our childcare worker, mother of three, took charge and with the help of other volunteer mothers, created our kids' play school. It was amazing what we did with empty toilet rolls, empty plastic bottles, wooden blocks and other rejects from building sites.

Our Women's House was able to be a central women's place where we could meet and make friendships and exchange advice. All the women with special skills made themselves available to other women in need. In general, the Women's House was a circuit breaker for most of us. Older women were stalwarts for young mothers who missed their mothers and families, and our house filled the niche.

*

There were other issues and we met all challenges head-on. Our own houses were fully furnished and had ghastly colour schemes; yellow walls with mustard-coloured lounges or blue walls with blue chairs or puke-coloured green. Some of the house-proud women found the colour combinations hard to cope with. I was not one of them but I did see their point of view. No changes to the colour schemes were allowed by the housing manager. The women became defiant and a stand-off was brewing. The Dampier library provided me with literature in which I found information relating to the negative effects colour can have on people's mental state. We wrote up our conclusions for what might happen as a result of mentally distressed women, and presented it to the company. They agreed to let the women alter their colour schemes. We had our second win!

*

It was 1970. A super-cyclone was pending, and we were advised to stock our pantries for at least several days. Women all headed for the general market. Belligerently, the grocery store manager in Dampier had doubled all the food prices. Angry women bailed up the manager, who merely said he could charge whatever he liked. Really! We'd see about that. Cyclone Sheila hit and our town was awash. After the weather had improved, we women met and made a plan.

The workers at the mining company were having a huge strike and a mass meeting was to be held at the Dampier community hall. I asked one of the union organisers if I could address the men at the meeting. The hall was full of tough-looking blokes and I was nervous but I argued that the men were going on strike for a few dollars on the one hand and the local grocery manager, by upping his prices to whatever he wanted, was taking their money out of their pockets with the other hand. If all the strikers would contribute one dollar or two, we women could organise our own food co-op and charter a ship for container of supplies up from Perth. We could then control the prices and save the men the money they were striking for. After the meeting, I had so much money thrown at me that I couldn't hold it all. I obtained use of a large steel container resting empty in the industrial site and located a Perth warehouse that would supply us with groceries, and that was the launch of our food co-op. We were independent, sufficiently effective for the manager of the major supermarket food store to complain to the mining management, which had guaranteed them a monopoly for twenty years…too bad about that!

*

One of my neighbours, Lorraine, organised for me to be employed as a barmaid at the Dampier Hotel. She was an experienced hotel worker and taught me how to be a barmaid. Union fees were deducted from my pay by the hotel and I assumed that made me a member of the union.

My reputation of organising the women at Karratha got around and I soon found women coming to me with work-related complaints. I became the 'shop steward' for the women workers.

Most of the mining workers were unmarried men and many spent their days off sitting and drinking at the bar. Gambling was the main entertainment and wild money, thousands of dollars, was spread out along the long counter during the days. Two flies crawling up a wall could cause the exchange of hundreds of dollars. There were daily brawls and when the local police officer had to go out of town he would leave the keys to the nearby lock-up cell with the hotel manager.

The mining company held an annual two-week shutdown for safety and maintenance checks of the gigantic machinery. Special tradesmen would arrive in the town to perform the maintenance and the pub did a roaring trade. The year I was working at the bar, our men had decided to stage a strike and it lasted into and during the shut-down period and when a horde of special tradesmen came into the pub at the beginning of their work time, I naively didn't know who they were and thought they must be scab labour brought in to break the strike. A wide sea of red-faced, bellowing, burly men poured through the big double glass doors, all struggling and pushing to get close to the liquid source of supply.

'Hey, luv, give us a big jug,' said a wiry man with long rusty tangled whiskers and a square bulldog jaw.

'Who are you blokes?' I asked.

'We're here to work for the shut-down.'

'Work?' I said.

'Work! This is a union hotel,' I said bravely. 'We don't serve scabs here.'

'Scabs!' he road at me. 'Who are you calling scabs?'

From my safety behind the bar, I stood my ground. 'You're scabs if you work on the job while our blokes are on strike.'

'Strike!' he yelled in disbelief. His billfold bulged like a barrel.

'Strike? What strike?'

The mob gathered around closer as I told them our workers were on strike.

'Hear that, comrades,' he called out. 'We can't go working on this job if our mates are on strike,' and a cheer rang out as they all agreed with him.

'Hear that, luv? Now give us a jug and keep 'em coming.'

My shop steward point having been made, I was happy.

*

I was aware, that, in those days, it was a common perception that women who worked behind the hotel bar would also prostitute for sex after hours.

'Don't worry. You'll be safe behind the bar,' my friend told me. 'These blokes know who's who.'

One day a woman from the other end of the long bar came to me with a complaint. 'That bloke in the dark shirt just propositioned me to have sex with him for forty dollars,' she said, all hurt and indignant.

I was mortified. Who did those fellows think they were? They couldn't just harass any respectable woman. I'd have none of that on my watch. I said I would complain to the manager and he would have him locked up for the night.

'Oh, no, luv,' she said. 'I don't want him locked up. I just want to know why he offered Jean to have sex for sixty dollars and only wants to pay me forty.'

My faced burned with embarrassment. A union issue, I mused? Equal pay for equal work?

*

Such was the reputation of women working behind the bar, any woman could be targeted.

'I'll give you five hundred dollars if you're wearing black knickers,' said a chap one day, and stacked five hundred dollars in front of me on the bar.

I was stunned, and then sniffed and ignored him, so he put another five hundred on top – a thousand dollars appeared.

'If you're wearing red knickers,' he said.

A thousand dollars! What sort of game was he playing? He would have to be kidding.

'Sorry.' I laughed nervously, not sure what the game was about. 'I'm married,' I said, hoping my husband would be on time to pick me up. Who would wear such vulgar red or black knickers? Miniskirts might be in, but who would show their undies?

After closing time, we workers gathered to partake of the customary after-work on-the-house drink with women from other parts of the hotel. We shared stories of events which had happened during the night and I told the other women about the bloke with all the money.

The women all giggled with glee and teased me mercilessly for being such a 'dumb twit of a prude'. OK, so red and black knickers were not so bad.

The next day, before time for me to start work, I went to the only shop that sold clothing and enquired about red or black knickers.

'I don't understand it,' the assistant said. 'You're the tenth woman to come in here today and I've completely sold out all the black and red knickers.'

I had a small giggle to myself and said, 'Well, you'd better get some more. It seems they're going to be a popular item around here.'

*

Another union issue arose that I felt I had to deal with. Many of the women who were employed to work at the hotel were flown up from Perth at the start of their employment. However, whenever a local woman was found to do the job, the Perth woman would be sacked, probably because she had to be paid union wages and local women were housewives, knew nothing of the proper wage, and could be exploited. A Perth woman would be sacked at the end of the day and would be evicted from her hotel accommodation immediately. Since the plane to Perth did not leave until the following morning, they often slept the night on the beach and were often raped or bashed and robbed. Many women were so afraid that they shared a bed for the night in the single men's accommodation. I brought this to the attention of the local United Trades Council and they took action, ensuring that the women were safely housed at the hotel until their plane left.

Because of all these union stances of mine, the hotel management saw fit to let me go and thus my barmaid-shop-steward time ended.

*

Living in the Pilbara in the last days of the 1969s was a daily challenge and required an ability to adapt. Many isolated women felt the need to be supportive of each other. As a group of women together, we were able to create services unthought-of when we first arrived. The most moving thing we undertook was to provide a burial service for one of our little preschool girls, who had died suddenly of kidney failure. Again, we were faced with an unusual situation. There was no provision for a ground burial. The surrounding area could not be dug up; it was all reserved for mining! The company owned the town and the company owned the land. It was their policy to return deceased persons back to the state where they came from. No one could be buried on a mining lease. Therefore, there were no coffins in the town, only air transport body bags. But in this case, the bereaved parents were intending to stay in the Pilbara and wanted their little girl to have a Christian burial close to them.

To have a burial, we needed a coffin and somewhere to bury the child. There were many carpenters on location but I chose to ask a young carpenter working on one of the houses to make a coffin suitable for a little girl. He told me he was honoured by the request and began straight away on a beautiful but sad little coffin.

I organised with the local shire for a place to bury the child in Roebourne, forty miles away. The women fitted out our station wagon with pretty, satin sheets and the children all made paper flowers as part of their play school activities. The tiny coffin was collected by Mack and he took it to the hospital. There, the doctor arranged the little girl into it. It was then delivered to the family home, where the friends of the family organised an appropriate Christian service as best as could be held in a home. Then they all followed us as Mack drove the station wagon to the burial site. Again, we assembled with heartbreaking sadness as we watched the little coffin being lowered into the rich, red sand close to a river bed.

*

Domestic violence was not something known to me in those days living in the Pilbara and, although I recalled my mother's words of advice not to let a man hit you, I was learning that violence and verbal abuse against wives and mothers was a private and secret affair. I heard women crying and saw women with physical evidence of the phenomenon but it was just how it was. No one said anything. I said nothing. We all kept our secrets to ourselves.

*

One day, my husband was called in to a management meeting and told to control his wife. At the time, he was scornfully amused. But his amusement faded one evening while he was waiting for me outside the grocery store. We topped up our supplies between our co-op shipments arrivals. It was a Friday night and there was a particularly long queue at the checkout. Mack was getting agitated but there was nothing I could do. We finally managed to load the car and were on our way, only twenty miles to home. We had to stop and wait at a train crossing. They were very long trains and it must have been about a ten-minute wait. Sometimes it was as long as twenty minutes before a heavy loaded iron ore train passed.

We crossed the rail line and out past Dampier, without any warning, Mack began to speed. He kept going faster and faster. I asked him to slow down but he just increased the speed until his foot was flat on the floor. The car could go no faster. There were no seat belts in cars then and the car swayed from side to side, all across the road. I was being thrown around in the front and the children were being tossed about in the back. I knew our lives were in peril. Then he steered the car on to the wrong side of the road, directly into oncoming traffic. I was terrified and once again my senses moved into high alert. We are all going to die.

I felt afraid. We were going to die. I had no idea what to do. I was helpless. I was being tossed around but I leant over the seat and told the children to get down and pack pillows and blankets around themselves as we raced at oncoming cars.

He screamed, 'I'll kill us all! I'll kill us all!' and I truly thought he would.

The car was travelling at breakneck speed. This could not end well, I thought, as his foot stayed jammed to the floor. We were on a straight stretch and I kept my eyes glued to the road, trying to anticipate when we were going to crash. Miraculously, the oncoming cars had time to pull over as we tore past. Further ahead, oncoming cars saw us coming and swerved to avoid us. Others pulled off into the bushes.

I experienced the most excruciating fear of my life. I believed there was no escape and we were all going to die. Instant dying would be all right. Being injured and unable to take care of the children was the main thought racing through my mind. I tried to stay calm but I was screaming inside. My thoughts were to pray and stay motionless, to stay calm. Really, I was frozen cold with fear and felt my blood had stopped running. I could do nothing. My head was tense and whirling, watching the road ahead, the flashing landscape whizzing past. I constantly glanced back at the children. I had no idea how far we were from home.

Then, suddenly, the car came to an abrupt stop.

No one moved. I thought we were dead. The children did not move from under the blankets. It was deathly silent, no sound at all. We had crashed without a bang. I heard no sound as he got out of the car. I thought we were dead and he was levitating, floating out of the car. Everything swirled slowly before my unfocused eyes.

He was back, yelling, 'Fuckin' get out of the car. Nothing happened. You weren't hurt.' Then he stomped off.

How could that be? I was confused. I thought if we wasn't dead, then where were we? His angry voice snapped me back to consciousness and I realised we were at home, in our driveway.

*

At the beginning of 1970, the Japanese economy altered and they responded by ceasing to buy further red rocks from Australia. Workers eagerly engaged a year or two earlier were now redundant. Some disgruntled employees returned home, others stayed. We chose to leave Western Australia. Mack was offered a voluntary termination package and accepted it.

In the summer of 1970, we loaded our trailer and drove back over the Nullarbor. We drove in the cool of the night because once again we were taking the trip in extreme heat.

A week later, we were back in Port Augusta.

3

1970–1974: I Rise to Feminism

I was glad to be home in South Australia. We settled not in Port Augusta but in Adelaide and bought a house in the then-safe Labor state electorate of Spence, and the federal seat of Hindmarsh. We reconnected with our past Labor Party associations. Mack joined the militant Builders' Labourers' Union and worked on several building sites around Adelaide. It was the time when Australia's participation in the Vietnam War was becoming unpopular and we as a family joined the growing voices and demonstrations of people who wanted an end to the war and an end to our young men being conscripted.

The three children were happily settled into a local primary school. They were good students, well-read and more knowledgeable about Australia than some of their teachers, having spent the last years travelling from one part of Australia to the other and seeing loads of things. My son's teacher once told me that every time she introduced a new topic he seemed to have read a book about it already. The children loved their school and performed well in their studies

But, even at this time, my young schoolgirl daughters were beginning to question the obvious discrimination against girls. 'Why can only boys do photography?' Jacquelynne asked. She challenged the school whenever it seemed to be operating unfairly. 'Why do I have to wash a man's shirt?' And my son, little as he was, protested strongly when boys were beaten with a cane. I challenged the school not to beat my son with a weapon or they would hear more from me. The children were encouraged to question unfairness, with reason or unreasonable tack, by their father, who seized every opportunity to take umbrage at a schoolteacher. He would expostulate on many and varied things in a way that would escalate simple school matters. We were always in conflict with the schools and the schools' inability to de-escalate the situation did not help. Mack was a master of conflict and manipulation and by the time the eldest was a high school student, her obsessive, hard-hat, slightly red socialist father had locked horns with her top hat blue Liberal family headmaster – two bull-headed obstinate males at loggerheads for several months. Finally their battle resulted in a Royal Commission in 1974. The outcome was summed up in a front-page newspaper headline: 'Trinity of Trouble.' Mack's response was simply that the commission showed more 'rhyme than reason' and he dismissed their findings.

When she was sixteen my much younger sister came to live with us to complete her final high school year. Our father thought girls didn't need further education, but allowed her to come and live with us to at least finish high school. Our poor working-class family struggled to keep the girls in high school books and uniforms and so my sister wore her previous country school uniform, adding to the city school's disdain of our family. 'If she can't afford our uniform, she should go back to where she came from!' We carried on in our support for her, adamant that a cultivated mind was more important than a dress code. She eventually finished her academic education with a science PhD. Our mother would have been proud. To their credit alone, living with a difficult turbulent and violent home life, all the children achieved well academically.

*

Women's cheap labour gave rise to a myriad of factory manufacturing work opportunities for women in the mid-1970s and I accepted employment in a canvas factory as a machinist. This position fell under the federal award of the Miscellaneous Workers' Union and I gladly accepted union membership. Within a very short time, I became our workplace shop steward.

'As a shop steward, it's your job to make sure your shop is safe for your members and see that notices for union meetings are posted on the noticeboard,' Jack Nyland, secretary of the Transport Union, advised me.

I was fine with matters of safety but with my absent education, writing up notices was another matter.

I was asked by the foreman to call a union meeting to have the machinist settle between them what months and dates they all wanted for their annual leave. I was nervous, but early in the morning I duly posted a notice.

UNION MEETING in the lunch room 2pm
To discuss your anal Leave
Annette – shop steward

A big ripple of giggles swept among the machinists. Even the sour-faced foreman took time to read the notice and walked around chuckling to himself. Then, the good-natured manager came out and read the notice. I thought I was in trouble but, no, he roared laughing, then the office girls came out one at a time and studied the noticeboard. They returned with their hands covering their mouths stifling their giggles. As ripples of giggles promenaded the factory floor, women vacated their machines and one by one paused to read as they passed the noticeboard on their way to the washroom. The shop floor was all in a twitter.

I wondered what all the fuss was about and took my turn to visit the washroom. I glanced at the noticeboard as I passed. There were no new notices, so what was all the fuss about?

'How was your anal leave, Annette?' some smart alec called out to me as I returned to my machine, and everyone roared with laughter.

My face turned bright red as the penny dropped. Spelling was never my forte.

The first week I started work, the radio was blasting out Woody Guthrie's song 'Union Maid' and it drove the foreman mad. He would rush to turn the radio down and the women all yelled, 'Turn it on, turn it on,' but he didn't, so the woman all sang the chorus loud and clear!

You can't scare me; I'm sticking to the union
I'm sticking to the union; I'm sticking to the union
You can't scare me; I'm sticking to the union
I'm sticking to the union
Till the day I die.

The new third verse by Nancy Katz was added and printed in the *Builders Labourers' Song Book* published in 1975:

A women's life is hard
Even with a union card
She's got to stand on her own two feet
Not be a servant of the male elite
It's time to make a stand
Keep working hand in hand
For there's a job that's got to be done
And a fight that's got to be won.

I like this verse. It is a constant reminder to me that we women still have much to keep fighting for.

In the 1970s, women's wages were seen as mere 'pocket money' and no thought was given to women who were trying to raise children on their own. Despite our 'lucky', wealthy country, many women often lived in abject poverty, unable to sustain themselves and their children on the meagre 'women's wage'. Among the many social issues that were galvanising women to action, nationally and worldwide, was 'equal pay for work of equal value'. There was strenuous opposition from men and, strangely, from some women as well. I took it upon myself to inform low-paid working women that times were changing and to encourage them to support the union cause.

Women were under-represented in unions. There were no women

organisers and no women were paid as officials. There were only women office workers who did the typing and, among other things, made the male officials their coffee. The campaign for equal pay was spearheaded by the trade unions and they needed robust membership to push their claims. Women worked two jobs, one at home without pay, where they worked long hours responsible for all the domestic cleaning, cooking and caring for children, and the other, where they were paid factory workers' 'pocket money', so they had little time to attend union meetings. Others did not see a union as something they should be involved with. It was men's business. And to my chagrin, women's membership in unions was low.

There were men in our factory, as well as many men in general, who did not support the claim for equal pay. 'I don't want my wife getting more money than me' was the common cry from a common man. My husband was not one of them. He was hugely supportive of my involvement in our union's struggle. I needed no push to be convinced. I still had clear in my mind the time when I was a fourteen-year-old girl in the back of a grocery store, being paid far less than the boys doing the easier counter jobs. Accordingly, I found great pleasure in taking part in a campaign for equal pay. I participated with jubilant energy.

*

That was not the only cause that took my attention while working in factories. As on-the-job shop steward, I was one day approached by one of the supervisors. He wanted me to talk with a woman who was crying at her machine. She would say nothing in the workroom so I took her to the lunch room to talk. She was injured and had some small bruises on her face and arms. She was in pain and her leg could not push the pedals on the big industrial machine. It took a lot of coaxing and patience before she let go small snippets of her trouble.

The contract we were working on paid a wage for a required

number of items sewn. After a quota was completed, any work item made over the quota was extra money. On principle (and because of my limited ability) I only ever made my required quota. She was a migrant woman with little English and she was one of the best machinists in the factory. She always exceeded her required quota; therefore, her pay was much more than the basic factory wage for women. It would vary from week to week according to how many items she was able to make. This payday, she was down on last week's take-home pay and her husband was not happy. Every week, her husband took her miserable 'pocket money' from her and complained it was not enough. Last night he had bashed her because she had brought home less money than last week. She was in a bad way at home. She told me he regularly bashed her and took away her money.

She slaved away at home caring for him and her children. She cooked and she cleaned and she was exhausted. 'I work, work, work. I clean, clean, clean. He bash me, bash, bash bash. Too much, too much!'

I was shocked. I had never before heard a woman who dared say she was beaten or forced to work at home.

Unwittingly, I thought, 'She's much worse off than me. My husband never takes my pay from me, he never demands domestic work.'

'Leave him,' I said to her.

'I no money. I no place go,' she said.

How stupid of me. Of course, she could not leave him. This woman was the first woman I met who talked about being bashed. I listened to her tell me about her life of violence and I immediately understood. I then knew that I was not the only one! But I had told no one about me. As I later travelled from job to job, I saw many working women who were abused and assaulted; I saw their bruises and the pain of their injuries. I assured myself they were much worse than me. The women did not have to explain. I knew. I saw they too had a secret. I began to see that what was happening to me was also happening to other women, not just one but many.

Still, I said nothing to anyone. As the maxim says, 'There's always someone worse off.'

*

After the canvas factory contract concluded, I was without a job, but work was plentiful and I deliberately chose to work in non-unionised places. I moved from one job to another, with a purpose. Unions needed strong memberships to support the equal wages claim but if a job had no union member employed at the factory, a union organiser could not enter the factory and invite women to join. With me as union member on the job, an official union representative had legal access to the factory where I worked. I frequently found myself with a week's pay in lieu of notice as I was regularly made 'redundant on the spot', regularly out of a job when the bosses found they had a unionist in their factory.

*

It was while I was assisting the unions to campaign for equal pay in 1972 that I came into contact with the women's movement, and once again my life took a different direction.

My union office had accepted a working women's group to display a notice for a meeting, the topic of which was 'equal pay for work of equal value'. I took note and visited the advertised address of the upcoming meeting. I wanted to visit before the meeting to be sure I had found the right location.

The meeting place was an immense, abandoned warehouse in Bloor Court in the city. It was the Women's Centre. The moment I walked through the dilapidated door with the orange paint peeling off, I was struck by a gargantuan culture shock. 'Lesbians are lovely' and 'With my speculum, I am strong!' and other similar messages on brightly vivid posters spouting rights for women were plastered all over the crumbling powdered walls. I thought some were crude and outright rude. 'What is a lesbian, what is a speculum?' I wondered with a perplexed mixture of curiosity.

In the big open space, many strange-looking women gathered. Some had flowing, unkempt hair with a matching, full-length, hippy-style dress. Others had very short hair or no hair at all. They were dressed like men, in trousers, with long flowering baggy shirts and some wore boots and leather jackets. All were young. These eerie looking women called themselves 'feminists'.

I felt passionately averse to the whole scene. I had never seen such vulgarity. Out of place and out of my comfort zone, I felt highly conspicuous in my miniskirt, pale stockings and high-heeled shoes. And yet no one there seemed dismayed by my presence. The woman at the front desk was warm and invited me to look around. I was in awe. I had never seen such a place. It was crammed with rhythmic lyrics of political messages that held my attention. 'What is this all abou?' I wondered, I decided there and then to return for the meeting.

*

A week later, I waded through an assembling throng of women and was directed to a smaller group gathering in a corner. This far section was furnished with several tapestry-clad big comfy plump chairs and created a cosy corner with a bookcase filled with stapled papers, books and magazines. I did not recognise any of the books. The small group of women were there to discuss the equal pay issue.

The women were very friendly and made me feel welcome. Apart from telling them my name, I contributed no opinions to the conversation and did not venture to speak that night. I just listened to what these weirdly dressed women had to say. They called themselves the Working Women's Group but to my surprise I learned that none of them worked in factories or any other permanent employment. They seemed to be floundering around the issues. There was no talk of union activism, no mention of state and federal awards, not even any mention of women factory workers for that matter! There was nothing about industrial relations laws.

I felt lost in their philosophical hypotheticals and the fact that they seemed to have no idea about real work issues. 'But,' I shrugged, 'what would I know? I'm just an uneducated factory worker, a married woman with school-aged kids and an extra one to boot.' Despite feeling out of my depth, I returned the following week, then the one after that and then again. Within a month or two, I was wearing blue jeans and leather boots, going to meetings and calling myself a feminist. I have been a feminist ever since!

I was initially intimidated by their education and was aware of my own lack of it. I felt conspicuous and afraid I would stuff up. I was afraid I would say something stupid. I was troubled as I listened to their eloquent vocabulary. I kept quiet, because no one needed to know that I could not write nor spell; that I did not know how to pronounce many words. That did not, however, stop me from going to their other meetings on childcare and abortion. I took a particular interest in their take on education in schools. I was concerned for my own daughters and young sister's education and learnt how most school curriculums favoured boys at even simple levels such as 'Dick's father was a pilot and Dora's mother was a housewife.' They called it 'sexism in education'.

They also raised awareness of sexism in employment. In those days, employment was advertised in daily newspapers under 'Men Wanted' and 'Women Wanted'. One such advertisement in the 'Women Wanted' section read, 'Personal secretary wanted. Be between 18yrs –30 yrs, prefer blond hair, must be attractive. Apply manager…'

The women from the Working Women's Group operating from Bloor Court would phone the manager and interview him. 'Do you have a full head of hair? Are you old with grey hair? Do you have clean fingernails? Do you have a beard? Sorry, I couldn't possibly work for an old man with a beard and grey hair!'

It was from these women that I learned about International Working Women's Day and I did all I could to learn about the history of women's emancipation, especially about women working in factories. 'Herstory' the women's movement called women's history. I participated in all the organised celebratory activities and took my young children along with me. I wanted my girls to know working women's history. I wanted them to know women once worked six days a week by their machines, delivered their babies there, and kept their sleeping babes alongside them for twelve hours each day. I wanted them to know it was women who first fought for a ten-hour working day by holding long hungry strikes, which later lead to the modern eight-hour working day. I wanted them to know working women had to fight for their right to vote, and for many other women's rights. I wanted them to know there was more than Jane Austen's women and her Mr Darcy. I was disappointed when the celebration of International Working Women's Day dropped the 'Working' and was renamed International Women's Day.

Despite their lack of current practical knowledge relating to factory work practices, the group did have a good grasp of the fact that women were a lowly paid source of cheap labour in workplaces. They seemed aware of the unequal division of housework chores and (lo and behold!) about wife-bashing. I was all ears but stayed quiet, asking only short questions. At that time, none of these feminists, among whom were openly self-professed lesbians, mentioned that wife-bashing could also be an issue in same-sex relationships. Women would not abuse other women, would they? Or perhaps these women kept their secrets too.

To me, it was an amazing new world of feminist language, songs and modern ideas, and they struck a chord in me. I was astounded that these young women were articulating many of the issues I had been mentally pondering and in time I became enthralled with their feminist political voice. I slowly overcame my shyness and sang along with them. 'Don't be too Polite Girls' was written by Glenn Tomasetti to note Australia's first attempt at equal pay – the 1969 decision for equal pay for equal work.

Chorus: 'Don't be too plite girls don't be too polite
Show a little fight girls, show a little fight
Don't be fearful of offending in case you get the sack
Just recognise your value and we won't look back.

*

The women's movement had been organising for about two years when I 'discovered' it. It was made up of mostly university students and graduates. They were an energetic group and in time I warmed to many of them. I was to learn that there were two obvious arms to this unofficial association. One group was known as the WLM or Women's Liberation Movement, while the other called itself WEL, the Women's Electoral Lobby.

The WLM group was made up of mostly young, radical, lesbian women. They were highly motivated to promote awareness of their sexual, political, social and domestic agendas for women. They tended to range from mild socialists to extreme communists. I was not daunted by that. I was confident in politics and shared a number of the WLM's social ideals. I did however feel some of their political ideology scattered, immature and lacking in substance.

The WEL tended to be more conservative older women. Their main political function seemed to be to canvas certain political candidates and members of parliament from all sides of the political spectrum. At election time, they handed out questionnaires relating to women's emancipation, they then compiled the results, distributed them and asked women to support the current member or candidate who held the best feminist attitude. They wielded quite some power and male politicians made sure their guards were up when they were visited by these women. Many failed the women's test.

The women's movement, in general, was officially 'free-structured', unlike the union movement with its strict boundaries of meeting rules and memberships and the similarity of the political party I was used to. The finances of the movement came from women who had the means

97

to give, and others who were not so well off also contributed. It was all done by donation. The women worked hard fund-raising and volunteering their time to keep the centre running. They were not having lamington street stalls but were promoting literature and articles written by progressive feminists. There was no 'boss', secretary, president and no membership fee, and no registration of participants. Mostly they gathered in groups to talk and had information-sharing sessions and consciousness-raising talks. Any woman could partake. The group decisions seemed to be made by consensus and they called their groups a collective. They did not want majority rule and democracy was out. It was, they said, the way men made decisions and the process left women out. As a group, it was 'everyone agrees or nothing happens'. I regarded this system as undemocratic folly. In practice, I found that consensus rule would cause the unit to function at the lowest common denominator. Admittedly it had a worthy base, in that no woman should be without fully understanding the issue at hand. No woman could be railroaded into a decision and decisions were not made until everyone totally understood and agreed. I felt, however, that the practice encouraged underhand bullying and wearing down by stealth of the weakest and least articulate.

In reality, the most articulate, strongest-willed woman with the strongest presence could influence a small number of devotees and lock them into her agenda, preventing decision-making that she did not agree with. Women began to agree with whoever had the most powerful position in the group. I was not deterred by this, but later paid the price for not sharing this consensus ideology and following the loudest voice. At regular meetings, larger groups dispersed into smaller interest groups where there was much opportunity for genuine and anxious talk, but they came together on big issues to discuss and reach a consensus. There were regular mass meetings and the alpha 'heavies' were a force to be reckoned with. Occasionally, when I voiced my opinion on a political matter, I won the day. At other times, I was frustrated by the group procrastination.

*

The women's movement was a valuable source of knowledge and offered women information on a variety of issues. I learnt a lot from these women, especially about women's history and their struggles for the vote. I was exposed to a wide variety of current women's issues and had a number of my own to share.

At the Women's Centre, there was a regular group of women who took it in turns at the telephone desk to take calls from other women seeking information or asking for accommodation to escape a violent situation. This group reported that there were bashed women walking the streets at night. Really! Hundreds of women rang anonymously. If they did not have to give their identity, they felt able to talk freely to another woman who was offering to listen. They could tell their 'secret'. They could ask for asylum, for a reprieve from their bashings. This phone information service was later funded by the state government and was based at a different location and called the Women's Information Service. They heard many wife-bashing stories.

The women's movement used the anonymous phone information to compile a lengthy written submission about bashings and the brutality of husbands and partners. For months they wrote letters, and dossiers flowed back and forth in both state and federal governments. They applied for a grant to purchase a house, and for extra funding to run a women's shelter. I sat through many frustrating meetings and listened to talk and more talk, then talk some more with no end in sight. It was not what I was used to. Isolated women in the Pilbara had had little time for talk. They had just got on and done it!

*

While all this was going on for me at the women's centre, other dramas were enveloping me at home.

After a night out to dinner it was usual for me to drive home if much wine had been consumed. I settled into the driver's seat and waited for Mack to arrive; he was not happy and insisted he drive. I was buckled in the car before we left and refused to let him drive, remembering the hell ride from the past. He grabbed the back of my hair and pounded my face into the steering wheel, again and again, but I would not budge from the driver's seat. Blood poured down my face almost blocking my vision when I finally got to drive home. The attack did not stop at the front door. He pushed me through and when I landed on the floor, blood from my face smeared the carpet, he kicked at me mercilessly. I tried very hard not to scream or cry out during these kicking episodes, as I did not want the children to hear their mother was being hurt. (How deluded I was.) Despite this, my head injuries were extensive, my body aflame with blunt trauma and pierced bleeding wounds. I should have had stitches in a gaping wound to my head but instead, I snuck into bed and nursed myself.

When the children got up the next morning, I had to sit in a chair while I apologised to them: this weekend I wouldn't be able to attend their Christmas party. 'How could I go looking like this?' I sighed. I could not escape their gazes.

They were upset to see me like I was, but they were sadly also used to it. 'What is she on about? I've seen her much worse than that,' is what I heard them whisper as I nursed my closed-up black eye and swollen upper arm.

Our home was a dark cloud of violent rolling thunder, held together by a string of odd-shaped beads; some bright, others dull, some bigger, some smaller. The only uniformity was the small knots between the beads.

In December 1973, Mack was accepted into Flinders University as part of their first intake of mature-age students. He enrolled for the 1974 academic year in politics and philosophy. And I was awakening to a new me.

*

By now it was 1974. I was elated by all the knowledge passed on to me by the women from the centre but I found that I differed from the women's movement in my opinions of what needed to be done about wife-bashing. The movement was in communication with male-dominated governments and was receiving no joy, but still they persisted, letter after letter, submission after submission. I was tired of the women's long drawn-out patience, their meeting after meeting, facing written requests for more information and still more requests. I wasn't interested in sitting around waiting for disregarding high-placed men giving us the run around. They did not care to see our poor working women's plight and I had no time for bureaucratic humdrum. I did not want to continue to appeal to uninterested males, giving them continuing power to refuse us via a flow of negative replies. I had other visions. To my simple but energetic mind, we women – 'we' being the women who were bashed – didn't need a super-duper big bureaucrat-run hostel for women to run to in the middle of the night. All we needed was a safe place to go when things got rough, a place run by understanding, soothing women, like my friend Iris back in my hometown.

This was the time when Jack Mundy of the New South Wales Builders' Labourers' Union was leading workers in running green bans. They were squatting in a long row of historic houses on the Sydney waterfront to prevent them from being demolished. The men and some women labourers were restoring the houses and offering them as secure, free and open places for the poor and homeless. It seemed to work for them.

So why couldn't we women squat in a government-owned house? I could see no reason, no reason at all, against this. There were plenty of strong, sturdy, abandoned houses sitting awaiting demolition right here in Adelaide. We could squat right there! The March women's movement meeting in 1974 was my goal. I would bring up the idea there.

By March 1974, I had attended many meetings of the women's

movement and I was starting to make myself unpopular by challenging the women with tougher stances. Their loyalty to their political parties or staunch strict feminist ideology and, in most cases, their academic education made them wary and unwilling to make waves and I questioned their will to support housewives and working women in need. I was an active member of a trade union and a member of the Labor Party but I was becoming more and more passionate and militant about the role of working women in our society, those at the very bottom of the economic scale. I was asking how we could effect change for them without having to ask men to help us and being constantly rebuffed.

My political involvement in the Labor Party had given me confidence, in that I understood the attitudes of men and I was becoming proficient in interpreting the language of the male-dominated unions and political parties. I was ever more sceptical of their desire to elevate women, of their stands on equality and of their desire for the emancipation of women. I heard blokes speaking in derogatory tones on the question of equal pay and other issues. For example, I heard sexist jokes from federal parliamentarians and found them flippant on important issues for women.

Politician 1: 'What do you reckon I should do about the abortion bill, Fred?'

Politician 2 : 'I dunno, Dave. I reckon you should pay it, old chap.'

This trivialising candour ended with bursts of laughter from their close-by audience.

Men thought this funny. I thought it condescending. Abortion was no laughing matter. Where I came from, girls as young as sixteen were burdened with motherhood and one girl I knew had four babies before she was nineteen because contraception was only available to married women and abortion was illegal for us all.

So I was not very hopeful that men in high places would help us, the women who suffered wife-bashing. I was hearing many stories from varied women. It seemed that no section of society was immune from wife-bashing but my heart was with the women who needed us in the middle of the night, the poorly paid factory workers or housewives who had no money and nowhere to go. We did not need a mansion, just a safe refuge. I was advocating that every suburb should have a women's shelter – a safe place for women to run to in the middle of the night.

*

The March women's general meeting was a lively one and well attended. I stood up to face a warehouse full of women from all areas of the economic spectrum. I took my turn to stand tall and face the full house; I spoke about the virtues of squatting and about bypassing our glib male 'supporters'. Then I faced the full barrage of cat calls of negative harangue. Oh dear. 'Squatting', I was to find, was a dirty word to the conservative, mostly middle-class, educated women. They were outraged, aghast at my suggestion. I was here now expecting to be lynched at the mere use of the word.

'You can't do that! We could all be arrested,' a loud voice declared.

'Are you mad?' someone cried.

'We could all get into trouble,' said another.

'We've just got a Whitlam government. We shouldn't do anything to upset them.'

There was unanimous 'consensus' voting all around me: no, no, no, no. Squatting was unthinkable.

I was appreciative of their concern for and support of the Labor government, but I was over it! Petulant men with long-held sexist views in controlling positions were keeping women poor and judging them unfavourably on their housekeeping, cooking and sexual performances, while the women suffered abandonment, bashings, eviction, homelessness and poverty, not to mention lowly paid work.

I left the meeting disheartened and isolated. Down but not out! The women's adamant insistence that squatting was not an option merely fuelled my enthusiasm for the idea. I knew better. My factory working friends (and I) needed a shelter now: winter was approaching and many cold nights were waiting for us night-time wanderers. So I put my union fight for equal pay aside for a while and set about finding a way to set up a women's shelter.

Adelaide had night shelters for men and rescue shelters for dogs and injured native animals – but nothing for injured women!

*

Unperturbed by the negative reactions from the women at the March mass meeting of the women's movement, I carried on in my own sanguine, unfettered way, determined to overcome the obstacles.

A house at Number 12 Torrens Road, Ovingham, was not far from my home and seemed to be silently sitting, waiting and calling out to be occupied. It was owned by the state government and held, in particular, by the Highways Department. It was earmarked for demolition in the long-term plans to upgrade major roads.

Thirteen-year-old Jacquelynne and I discovered the house when we were out searching. The broken window and the dried-up, overgrown tall grass out the front were like a beacon and begged us to take a closer look. Its location was ideal: on the main road for safety and with no neighbours to detect us before we were securely ensconced. And it was obvious enough for women to easily find us. The house was a big, old, solid, bluestone dwelling with a strong, heavy front door that could be seen clearly from the busy main road. It had been a typical, modestly grand Adelaide residence, about late-1880s style.

I drove past, went around the block and back again and then drove up the side, close to the house, around to the back. The house next door had already been demolished and there were plenty of parking spaces. Closer inspection of the backyard showed an outside toilet. The water meter had been turned off and, because someone had used the toilet, it was off-putting but nothing that a bottle of Jasol cleaner and some disinfected rubber gloves and a good scrub couldn't fix.

The back door was swinging loose and, as I pushed the door warily, it swung open with a squeak. Cautiously we crept inside. We looked all the way through the house, and on first appearances it looked promising. Just inside the back door were two small rooms. To the left there was a kitchen, complete with oven and kitchen sink. I picked up a table and three chairs that had tipped over. They were sturdy and serviceable. Directly across the passage was the bathroom, with a huge, deep bath, a hand basin and an electric water heater. Further in, two more small rooms faced each other. One I was already mentally putting aside for an office or quiet room for talks, and the other held a treasure of a huge, open fireplace. In the front of the house were four big rooms, two on each side of a very wide and long passage. In places, hand-sized pieces of plaster were falling from the walls. That didn't matter. 'Hang a picture there' was my thought.

We sneaked along the passage with some trepidation. It was a big, empty house and felt spooky. My co-intruder suddenly stopped. She had heard something, a sort of whining. I heard nothing but when she turned to run, I was right at her heels. Before we got to the back door, a family of cats – mother, father and several kittens – raced us out. So much for brave squatters! We laughed at the ridiculousness of being chased by a hoard of little kittens.

On returning to the front rooms, we found one had a dirty mattress and old rags lying around in it. Several wine bottles were scattered about. The central passage had a solid wooden door with a big keyhole to spy through. All the floors were polishable bare boards. (The squat house appeared to be in better condition than my own family home, which had been slowly damaged; one internal door had its decorative glass broken while the other I had mended with hard plastic sheeting.)

The damaged abandoned house had no faults that could not be overcome. I was ecstatic. We had found our women's shelter!

*

I was determined to set up a women's shelter in this crumbling house. But reality told me that I could not hold a squat alone and realised I would need the support of others to hold the fort once we were in. I was alone and had no one to stand with me so I went back to the Women's Centre, hoping to find someone who might back me. I did not want the whole women's movement to be involved nor did I want them to put their reputations at risk. No one seemed to be willing to step outside of the consensus of the group.

Cautiously I approached a big, powerful, influential, young, educated lesbian woman who wore a leather jacket and rode a big motorbike. She was Jane. She appeared fearsome, and I felt intimidated by her, but I wanted support. She had influence in the liberation movement. I mistakenly thought she would be of the 'left'; kind, militant and undaunted. She had many friends. I approached her and asked if she and her friends were prepared to be involved in a squat. At first, she refused. I talked some more and eventually she agreed to ask around.

Jane came back to me with a proposition. 'I would have asked the Minister for Highways, Geoff Virgo, for permission to squat.'

Permission to squat? I was dumbfounded. Could this highly educated, intelligent woman really be so naïve? No one in government, no one on either side of the political field, would be silly enough to give a bunch of women 'permission' to shelter in a crumbling, less-than-desirable property. Besides, squatting was against the law and who would give 'permission' for an illegal occupation?

'That won't happen,' I said as I looked at her quizzically.

'Well, that's my condition,' was her answer. She wanted the safety of permission to use the house. She explained that she came from an old Adelaide family with a respectable name and could not have her name associated with something as socially unacceptable as squatting. I understood the issue of 'respectability' very well. I had lived shame, I was a nobody without influences and I had nothing to lose, So...

Feeling let down but undaunted, I squared up to her and said, 'I'll be squatting in three weeks' time,'and set the moving-into-the-squat day for Sunday 2 June. I innocently believed that I could still find someone to squat with me and would even go it on my own if I found no one.

A few days later, she got back to me and said she had willing women on board. She had two women Sally and Lue, close friends who were immediately willing, and was sure others would volunteer as time went by.

*

Meanwhile, Jacquelynne and I returned the squat house and spent many after-school days cleaning and sweeping making ready for the start-up day. My younger daughter also took part in the pre-open day clean-up and both girls worked harmoniously to make the derelict house ready.

The time came when I had to tell Mack what I was planning, about my intention to squat. As I was about to embark on an unknown, true to the behaviour of a victim, my first thought was how my actions would affect my abuser. I chose my time of announcement with care. It was weird for me to be talking to him about women who were bashed and in need of shelter, without me relating it to myself or him as a violent person. I told him I was going to set up a shelter for women escaping wife-bashing. I told him I was going to squat in a house. He was highly amused!

Of course, I did not say it was partly self-interest, and because I myself needed somewhere to run. The shelter would surely be my refuge at some time, I thought, but it never occurred to me that I might ever need a permanent place of refuge. It was my thought to use my maiden name, so he could not readily be connected and so would not be shamed if I failed or was put to public ridicule and disgraced.

'What do you think?' I asked. I was surprised at how supportive he was.

'No need to change your name,' he said. He launched into a long, political, socialist oration and let loose with a string of his favourite superlative moralities. 'Silence is not golden, it is yellow and yellow is the colour of cowards. No member of my family will be a coward…' et cetera. 'It would be cowardly not to speak out against women being bashed…'

I gulped! Other people's wife-bashing, that is, not his, not mine. Yes, it was weird. He was supporting me to squat, knowing I was going to be supporting women like myself who were being bashed and abused. He was supporting me to publicly condemn men who bashed women and children – like he did. But it was a secret, so he held no fear. He knew I would not tell. As part of abuse, abusers are confident that with their 'control' and silence, the secret is assured.

I now know that this attitude of his – to be helpful – is common to that of an abuser. Abusers often refuse to self-identify as the perpetrator, an assailant of violence or child sexual abuse. Once the violent deed is done, it is done and not talked about or even acknowledged in any way. Sceptic that I am, I always look askance at people, especially men, who strongly and loudly oppose domestic violence. To my mind, they are just as likely to be abusers. One never knows.

*

Plans for the shelter were at hand. I felt confident but also afraid of what might happen, and unconfident of the willing women. I was aware of the big political risk we were taking. Would we be evicted in a blaze of infamous publicity? Would I – we – be arrested? The Pilbara had been different. There we had been a multitude of women in harmony and here I was alone with unquantified jittery women and had to tread softly.

The word was quietly circulated that women were taking a stand against wife-bashing. I put a call out to charitable organisations (without letting out too much information) for donations of furnishings, household goods and all things we could use to make up a house to accommodate women and children. The response was overwhelming. I stored stuff and furniture on my front veranda and was confident we had enough to begin operating.

I heard Mack telling someone in a joking sort of way, 'You can't miss our place. It's the one with tables, chairs, beds and junk piled high out on the front veranda.'

*

Early in the morning on Sunday 2 June 1974, complete with husband and children, I arrived at 12 Torrens Road. We went through the back door and did a quick last-minute run through and tidy up, taking mental note of repairs and jobs that would need to be done. Mack had brought his tools and a small amount of building materials to make the minor repairs needed for basic security. Being able to secure the main entrance was important, so he fixed a super-strong barrel-and-bolt locking mechanism to the front door.

As early as nine a.m. people began arriving, bringing household furniture and other equipment they thought we might need. They helped make the rooms ready for occupation. They patched broken windows, folded bedlinen and set about repairing whatever they found broken. During the day, the house took on a party atmosphere, with many strangers coming to wish us well. I was overwhelmed and exhilarated by the support. Women arrived and capable strong lesbian women joined the frolic, armed with tools and heavy gear. It was a momentous occasion.

All day long, men and women arrived with blankets, crockery, in fact everything imaginable, to provision a house. There was hammering and banging and lawnmowers and garden tools screaming as people tirelessly fixed this and that and cleaned up the front yard.

The day was sunny but cold and so I lit a big, cheery, welcoming fire in the huge, open fireplace. I did the 'meet, greet and thanks' and as things arrived, I directed where the stuff should go. Before long, the warm lounge room was set up with comfortable sitting spaces and people gathered with copious cups of coffee. Woman sang their feminist songs, the whole day was high energy, and a joyous jamboree, as good wishes flowed freely.

My youngest daughter fussed around, colour coordinating the rooms for no reason other than to look orderly. She made the rooms pretty by putting pink bedspreads in one and blue in the other. My eight-year-old son sorted and packed toys and books for the children. And visiting young girls delighted in folding and stacking the clean clothing that had been donated into the wardrobes. The most unusual and unexpected donation that day was a small carton of Abiscol cream.

'It's for scabies,' the donor said.

'What is scabies?' I asked. 'I've never heard of scabies.'

'You'll soon know if you get them. They're small mites that get under your skin.'

Another gift was a very inspirational and emotionally uplifting sign, hand-painted onto a beaten piece of flattened tin. It had on it the big women's circle with the cross and read, 'Women's Shelter'. It had been painted by the brother of the woman who delivered it and women helped nail it to the stone and rubble front fence. It made a classic statement and summed up a brilliant day. We were done. The sign announced to all that women had taken over the house, a house for all women. Nothing shy or secret about it! We were here and we were not going away!

*

After the crowd had left and all was quiet, I was left to worry about the next twenty-four hours. I was concerned about what the reaction would be when we were discovered by the authorities. Would the police be called? Who would be the first to discover us squatting? What would they do about it?

On that first night, Jane, who was the most outspoken WLM, Sally and Lue, also members of WLM, from the Women's Centre, held a meeting of a group of other WLM women. They huddled by the cheery fire in the lounge and set out a plan for how the shelter would be run. A roster was drawn up and it was proposed that women would volunteer what time they could. It was my experience that rosters and volunteering would not provide a reliable, functioning system, especially as the young women had their education, professional careers and futures to consider. I was sceptical and knew that enthusiasm often waned quickly after the initial excitement had worn off. But for this night, it was most important to be vigilant and claim possession of the house; the running of the shelter could be sorted at a later date.

Jane and Sally agreed to stand guard in the squat on the first night and Jacquelynne asked to be allowed to stay with them. I let her, because the women were responsible schoolteachers and I thought it would be a pleasant memory for my daughter when she grew up, to be able to say that she had made a stand for women and children against wife-bashing. As it happened, more children than women were to occupy our women's shelter. However, the night did not go well for Jacquelynne.

As it was getting dark, Jane and Sally left the house to buy takeaway food for tea and Jacquelynne was left alone in the house by the fire with only the light of one candle. As the cold night raced to darkness, the house became a cave of shadowy figures in the flickering candlelight. The back door banged and rattled in the cold wind as it whistled around the house. A light rain beat through one of the broken windows. On just such a night, the scary spooks come out! It was not a night for a lone child to be without adult protection in a dark deserted house and poor tiny Jacquelynne was petrified. Was someone trying to get in? Were those figures in the lightning flash real? Was there anyone there?

When there was a pause in the noises, she tiptoed to the front door and put her eye to the large keyhole. Her panic turned to horror when a huge eye on the other side of the door looked straight into her eye. Some homeless men had come back to their nightly place to kip. She screamed and ran for the back door, out of the house, down the hill and straight into the arms of the returning women.

Jane delivered a still-distressed child home on the back of her motorbike on Monday morning in time for school. I was fuming at the irresponsibility of the women as my daughter told me of her night of terror. No one should have been left alone in the dark, derelict house, let alone a small child. I was in despair. We were supposed to be caring for people, not abandoning them to fear. In my mind, I seriously questioned her sense of responsibility.

*

We had lost our family car in a motor accident in April a few weeks before the shelter opened. Mack bought a small scooter motorbike, enabling him to travel to the university, and I resurrected my bicycle and pedalled my way around until we could locate an affordable vehicle.

On Monday 3 June, the next day of the squat, after my children had gone off to school, I tenaciously loaded my bike with bits and pieces from my kitchen, a large frying pan and a pocketful of twenty-cent pieces, and pushed my way uphill to 'our' women's shelter. I set about cleaning out the fireplace, emptied the overflowing ashtrays and cleaned the coffee cups left by all the willing volunteers and well-wishers. I lit the fire again. We had plenty of firewood because someone had delivered a big pile to the backyard. I intended to keep a warm fire going so that anyone who arrived would find the house warm and cosy.

I then checked the kitchen supplies and sorted out some more donations. After ten o'clock, I skittered down to the phone box on the corner and rang all the possible referring agencies, letting them know that we had a shelter for women and children needing accommodation. Any woman or child could come at any time of day or night and there would be no fee.

I also rang the Electricians Union and said we were in, without electricity.

'Right,' was the one-word reply.

*

Later that next morning, more people arrived and brought beds and other equipment and, to my amazement, handed me money. I had never expected money donations and had made no banking preparations. I put the dollars in a jar in the wardrobe in the small room allocated to be the office.

That very first day, late in the afternoon, a woman and her preschool daughter arrived. That shocked me: an arrival, so soon and during the day. I only wandered around at night. The woman told me her name was Jeanie and her daughter was four-year-old Sharon. Jeanie had rung Lifeline only hours after I had phoned them and they gave her our address. Fussed and bothered, I was unsure of what to do or say. Meeting my first woman stranger, gently sobbing, was daunting. However, the warm fire and a pot of tea and biscuits soon put us at ease and before long we were chatting like old friends.

Jeanie seemed not to notice the dimness of the house. She was just grateful to have somewhere to go. Her words alone were enough for me to feel justified in squatting. I asked her no questions and she only said she wanted to get away from the man who was bashing her. Both Jeanie and her little girl had slept outdoors the previous night.

'What, in the rain?' I asked.

'No, in a school lunch shed,' she answered.

Ah yes, I thought, of course, that was a favourite place for us women to seek shelter. I was to hear this story repeated many times over the next few years: women and children walking the streets at night and finally dossing down in school yards. Seems like that was what we all did in those days. But I never took my children with me, thinking they were safe in their beds at home. Safe? Little did I know!

Jeanie said she was not going back. She had left many times before, had even once ended up in hospital but had always gone back. Now she had found a place here, she was not going back. Could it be that easy? I wondered – but then I had never been bashed badly enough to end up in hospital, or was that because I just did not go?

I had to tell her we were squatting and were not legitimately here. She was not in the least fazed. In fact, she was delighted to be able to be of help. All the fuss I had made in looking for someone, anyone, to help run and organise the shelter and the answer was here all the time: build up the shelter and women would come, and who could better run the place than the women who used and needed it? In the weeks and months that followed, it was the women who did not go back to their husbands who organised the working structure and set the policies of the shelter.

That night, I was relieved by a volunteer from the women's movement who arrived to stay for the night with Jeanie and Sharon. Fortunately, there were no visits from homeless men. My terrified daughter's screams may have done the trick.

*

On the Tuesday morning, I pedalled hard up the hill in light rain to find, on arrival at the shelter, that Jeanie had the fire going and a pot of tea waiting. We sat by the fire and talked for a long while about the injustices for women and how hard it was for women to find accommodation. There was no welfare money that would provide enough for rent and Jeanie had accepted unhappy, live-in housekeeping positions where she had ended up being raped by the house owner. But now she felt new hope.

Positions as live-in 'housekeeper' for deserted men were the most common source of accommodation for women escaping violence in those days. It appears the men were abusers and their wives had fled. Many unsuspecting young attractive homeless women fell victim to these recidivist unknown abusers.

During Tuesday day, our second woman arrived. She was middle aged, her hair was a tangle mess of grey knots and her sagging sun-toughened face was brown with deep ageing furrows. She wore several layers of tattered and dishevelled clothing. Her teeth were black and yellow and she had a bad smell. She was not clean and, after a quick talk, headed for the shower. The water was cold but she seemed not to care. Jeanie found soap, toothpaste, brush (from the many donated items) and a towel and when the woman was finished, she fumbled through the donated clothes for clean, warm things to put on. Then she joined Jeanie and me by the fire for tea and toast.

She said her name was Maggie and she was homeless. Maggie had divorced her husband (who she said was a bad man) many years ago. 'Welfare took me kids orf me and I never bin the same since.' She had no money and just survived hand to mouth. There were no pensions for lone women in those days and she just coped the best way she could.

'Did ya know, luv,' she looked at Jeanie, 'them duck eggs from along the Torrens River are free and really tasty. Ya just stick a hole in 'em and suck.'

Jeanie's eyes widened. 'No, I didn't know that,' and she held back a laugh.

'And where did you sleep last night?' I asked.

'Under the bridge, but y' know, luv, it got too crowded, too many fellas. You know what that means?' she said to me with a wink.

Maggie always went to the local drop-in centre for the homeless during the day and they had driven her to us. They said she was getting a bit too old to be sleeping out. She had taken to drinking. It dulled the memories and took the edge off the cold. Jeanie and I looked at each other, our ears agog with her stories. There were night shelters for men and refuges for homeless or injured dogs, but nothing for women – they slept outdoors.

Many older women would be regular short-time residents at our shelter. They were the victims of wife-bashings of years gone by. They were left homeless, lost their children to welfare and slid into poverty. They would turn to alcohol and wander around the streets begging. Commonly known as bag-women, there were many, I was to learn and there was little support or concern for them. They were out of sight and many out of mind. They were our country's unknown undesirable and our 'untouchables'.

That Tuesday afternoon, Mack arrived. He had two J-shaped pieces of flat iron with three holes drilled in each and a long, thick plank of wood. He bolted the J-shaped iron brackets one on each side of the back door and jammed the thick board across the panelling then into the brackets. It was strong. It was good. It felt safe. The shelter was now more secure and I was confident that our front and back doors were adequately secure.

Another volunteer arrived to stay with the women for the night and I did not return until the next day.

*

There were no new arrivals during the night but in the early morning just after I arrived for the day, a woman with two little girls not yet school aged holding tightly to her skirts appeared in the passage, apprehensive and agitated. She was constantly looking behind her. I introduced myself and she said her name was Rose. She asked how much it would cost for her to stay. I was taken aback. I had not considered this question, as I had told the referring agencies that there was no fee. There had been no conversations about payment for staying so I told Rose that it did not cost anything but if she could contribute something, it would be welcome.

She opened her tiny money bag and said, 'Could I please have six dollars-worth of safety?'

Oh, such a miserable sight, oh so heart-rending. How could I possibly have said such a thing to a woman clearly distressed and seeking asylum in our humble abode? I felt deep regret for being so mindless. I spontaneously put my arms around her as she began to cry. My hand covered her hand of jangling coins and I shook my head. 'No, no,' I said.

'I saw your sign on the front fence. I've left my car on the road out front. I'm scared my husband will be following, looking for me. He'll see my car and follow me in,' she said.

With a learned sense which had become my natural impulse to threats of danger, I sprang into action. Leaving her standing in the passage, I rushed to lock the front door, then whizzed to the back door and put up the barricade. Jeannie came out to see what the flurry was about but she needed no explanation when she saw Rose and the two girls. She immediately took them into the warm room, where Maggie had tea and toast ready. We chatted for a while then Rose drove her car up the driveway and parked it out of sight close to the back door.

I was to learn that it was an excellent way to operate a women's shelter – women caring for other women in the purest most practical form. It was what I had envisaged.

*

Rose's story was the first I had heard of wife-bashers also sexually abusing children.

'I work night shift in a biscuit factory,' began Rose as she realised she had willing listeners. 'I drive to work every night of the week. When I got home from work this morning, he accused me of having an affair with the foreman. He said he saw me get into his car, which I didn't. Then he followed me home. He started slapping me. It's not the first time. He has bashed me often. I slumped into a chair and waited for him to take Jenna my seven-year-old, to special school. She's a bit retarded. When he left, I quickly grabbed the girls' clothes and piled them into the car. He really scared me when he reckoned I was having an affair – he said he'd kill me – so I drove around and around and didn't know where to go. I was scared he'd follow me. He always follows me. Then I saw the sign outside and came in. I know he's sexually abusing Jenna. I went to welfare and told them but they said I had no proof, they said that he was a lovely man and that I'm a vindictive wife. I don't know what I can do for Jenna. He'd kill me if I tried to take her from him. He says he'll kill me. I can't go back.'

This story was repeated often in the ensuing months. Women who reported child abuse within their marriage to the police or welfare were not received well. Some were accused of lying to make their husbands look bad. Women like Rose were rarely believed.

*

Rose's story gave me my first knowledge of child sexual abuse. It was something I never considered could happen in any home I knew. Throughout my childhood I had never come across anyone whose father would consider such a thing. No way would Mack do anything like that to his children. Clearly, men who did that were disgusting demons. These poor women were indeed much worse off than me.

Later that first Wednesday afternoon, a man came to the door. The women called me and took themselves into the safety of the warm room, out of sight. Through the spyhole in the front door, he looked an unthreatening figure in work clothes. I gingerly opened the front door.

'You havin' trouble with your electricity?' he asked.

'Yes,' I answered.

'Do you know me?' he asked.

'No.'

'Good. I'll just have a bit of a look at your meter box,' he said, fiddled a bit and then, 'You don't know me. You never saw me.'

'Right,' I nodded and he worked outside the house for another half hour or so and then left.

Such was the generosity of strangers who we did not know but were willing to assist us. Their help was inspiring, and we were very grateful.

That night we had electric lights and kitchen power points and next day, hot water in the bathroom. We could probably have done without the day's mysterious shenanigans because when I went out, I found, tucked in the meter box, an application for electricity and gas that I had not noticed before. All it had needed was for me to fill in some forms. I took the empty form and filed it in the office.

We also had just enough cash from donations to apply for a telephone connection and so I sent off for the necessary form. When it arrived, I looked at it: 'Tenant Name: previous address.' I wondered how to fill it out, decided it could wait a while and simply filed it with the electricity form.

The house walls were brightened by women from the volunteer group with posters proclaiming, 'Sisterhood is powerful', 'Lesbians are lovely', 'and with my speculum I am strong' and 'Wonder Woman'.

*

By the end of the first week, we had five women and eight children in the house. Jeannie and Rose, who were to be our first long-term residents, were both taking a leading role in meeting and greeting new arrivals. I accompanied Rose in her car back to her house to collect more clothing and some blankets while her husband was out. I escorted many women back to their homes to collect items they needed, such as bank books, marriage certificates, children's birth certificates and passports. (These documents were needed for future legal matters.) Having support while collecting possessions was a big part of the help they needed in those days.

*

On the first Sunday afternoon of our squatting takeover, and then every Sunday afternoon thereafter, Jane, Sally and Women's Liberation friends rode their motorbikes into the backyard and parked among the accumulating rubbish bags. They called themselves a 'collective', held their collective meeting in the lounge room and invited the residents to join them – but they preferred to stand in the passage and listen in. The meeting participants settled by the cosy fire. Jane was obviously the unofficial leader; she led by her striking physical powerful presence, and her eloquent and competent speech. She spoke of feminist ideals and consciousness-raising. The resident women's eyes glazed over.

Then they got on to what needed to be done at the shelter. Volunteers from the collective were not keeping up their promised commitments. Some voices piped up that they did not know what to do when they did appear and that the residents wondered why they had come. The remedy was a day book in which each volunteer would record events so that the next volunteer could see what had been happening.

When the meeting concluded, they packed up, rode their bikes over the rubbish bags and went on their way. The residents picked up the coffee cups, cleaned out the ashtrays, washed up and later raked up the scattered rubbish.

During that third week of the squat, Mack came and fixed a window and repaired some other hanging doors. As he was leaving, one of the WLM volunteers arrived with the day book. She asked what there was for her to do and I said there were sheets from some 'overnighters' to be hung out to dry. Well! She huffed and puffed and grumbled that she was not there to be a domestic for anyone. She was there to help women. She tried sticking a few posters back onto the powdery limewashed walls before going into the lounge to talk with some women. Then, before she left, she wrote up her activities in the day book, adding as a complaint that I had allowed a man (Mack) into the shelter.

On the fourth Sunday, Jane held court again in the lounge room with ten or so members of the WLM collective. Women residents were again invited in, but they stayed in the passage and peered into the room to observe. The collective members in the lounge chatted for a long time and expounded on the virtues of the day book. I had not written in it and it had been noted.

The meeting came around to the legality of the squat and what should be done about the utilities account. My long-held champion Jack Nyland, secretary of the Transport Workers' Union, had been cautiously supportive when I first talked to him about squatting. He instilled in me that we had to make sure squatting was all we did 'illegally'. With all other matters from then on, he said, we should do everything legitimately. So it was with his good advice in my mind, not to mention my own thoughts precisely, that I raised the question in the meeting about the accounts. It did not go as I expected and I was stunned and mortified by Jane's incredible suggestions.

Jane said that all accounts were to be put in false names so that no one single person would be held responsible. If the bills did not get paid and the supply company came looking, they would find no one. To my chagrin, every one of the collective present that day agreed with her. I was appalled. I would have none of that. We would be dismissed as irresponsible and downright dishonest. I suggested a compromise; that the electricity, telephone and gas accounts be registered thus, one account in Jane's name, one account in my name and one in Sally's.

Sally was Jane's 'lieutenant', one of Jane's comrade in arms support women who Jane kept close to lend support for her proposals.

Jane was outraged that I would suggest an alternative to her idea of anonymity for all. She was adamant that no account would bear her name or the name of anyone in the collective. Jane said she came from a well-known respectable Adelaide business family and if the accounts did not get paid, she could not have the shame of bad debts in her name. The meeting ended with no decision about the accounts.

Shame and debt be something I was used to. I felt no choice but to accept financial responsibility and registered all the accounts in my name and hoped I could find the money to pay them when the bills came in.

This infuriated Jane and she boiled with frustration towards me. I no longer felt intimidated by her: dishonesty of this nature has never had favour with me.

It was at this point that I knew things were very wrong about this set-up. It confirmed my thoughts that their feminist consensus system allowed the strongest and most powerful voice to control and deliver her agenda. No woman spoke against the consensus decision for fear of rejection and ridicule. Jane alone was the 'collective strength' and the force that the other women in the collective would follow. I meanwhile saw my feminist ideology sitting well with that of trade unions to care for the workers. I was not working for and not with the radical feminists, but with grassroots women who needed shelter. I already knew that this would be only the first of many clashes between me, and Jane and her loyal collective supporters.

Anne Summers, in her book *Ducks on the Pond,* referred to the Women's Liberation Movement and their method of operating:

> …we had unwittingly produced structures that were more insidious because they were less accountable. The loud and the bold could dominate and wield power in a most undemocratic fashion. It seemed to many, that we did have leaders, it was just that we did not admit it.

The meeting finally ended, the collective left and the residents and I cleaned the room of cigarette ash, butts and coffee cups. The bikers once again rode their bikes over the rubbish bags, spreading more mess, and we were again left to clean up the sprawling filth.

The residents were not happy. 'Why are "those women" here?' was the question they asked.

*

We were into fourth week when one of the resident women came running. There were two men in suits banging on the front door. The banging was urgent. It sounded serious. Was it the police in plain clothes?

'Quick! Get everyone inside and barricade the back door,' she directed.

The women and children scurried together and took refuge in the warm room. The curious kids all ran to the front room and pressed their noses to the window to look, giggling and squealing in shrills of delight.

Satisfied that all the women were safe and the back door was secure, I crept up the passage and waited behind the front door. The banging kept on. I thought I would wait them out but no, they would not go away. I would have to face the music.

Suddenly I flung open the door. That startled them! I had taken them by surprise and they jumped back. Then they just stood there and looked at me in dismay.

'Good morning, gentlemen,' I said as politely as I could. We might have been unruly squatters but there was no need to be unpleasant.

They returned my greeting and I stood waiting for them to say something. There was a long pause. It seemed they did not know how to start.

Then one said, 'Are you renting this house?' to which I answered, 'No.'

The other said,' Are you buying this house?' to which I said, 'No.'

Then it was back to the first bloke. 'Are you leasing this house?' to which I said 'No' and thought, 'This game is getting interesting!'

The blokes took a long pause and stepped back, whispering to each other. Then they stepped forward and one said, 'This house belongs to the Highways Department,' and their raised eyebrows and slight lean forward told me it was more a question than a statement.

'Yes,' I admitted.

Bill and Ben were taking it in turns to ping-pong speak. 'Do you have permission to be here?' to which I answered, 'No.'

They were gobsmacked. They stepped back for another mini-conference. By this time, several curious women had gathered up close behind me. They were giggling at these two ganders scratching their brains at our door. But they were not done. They were going to get to the bottom of this!

'Well,' said one, 'if you're not renting, you're not buying and you're not leasing and you don't have permission to be here, what are you doing here?'

I took a deep breath and with a cheeky grin said, 'We're squatting.' As bold as brass! It was so funny to see the looks on those men's faces. They were stumped.

'We're women and children who are taking a stand against wife-bashing.'

'Your turn,' I thought. 'What are you going to say to that?' As they rubbed their chins in thought, then it occurred to me that I didn't even know who they were.

'And so, who are you?'

At this, they jumped into gear, straightened their ties and slowly said, 'We're from the council. No one asked us permission to put a sign on the front fence. You require council permission to put up signage. You'll have to apply to council for that sign.'

I couldn't believe my ears. We had taken over a house without authority and they were merely asking us to get permission to put a teeny, weeny, rough sign on a fence. They had to be kidding!

'No, I won't be doing that!' I answered cheekily.

They looked aghast. No one said no to important men from the council. They spluttered and stammered and just kept standing there.

'You two gentlemen should be grateful to these women.' I swelled with confidence. 'They're choosing your council to be the first council area in Adelaide to establish a women's shelter. You should show your appreciation by sending your garbage trucks round to collect the rubbish which we found in this derelict house when we cleaned it up for you!'

They managed to open and close their mouths but no words came out, only grunts that sounded like 'Er, er we'll see what er er can do er,' and off they went. They couldn't disappear quickly enough. In those days, women simply did not talk back to men with council influence.

No truck came for the accumulating rubbish but the council never bothered us again. I learned later that we were much talked about at subsequent council meetings and that there was quiet, cautious support for us. We had no more trouble from the council.

And so, to the media. The following day, another young man knocked at the door. I applied the same caution as I slunk to the door. He was alone, so I stepped out to talk with him.

'What's going on here?' asked the smart, young journalist. He had seen our sign on the front fence and wanted a story.

I was reluctant to talk to him without consulting the women, so I told him I would think about it over the weekend.

Next Sunday meeting, several women from the collective squeezed around the warm fire the resident women organised and held their meeting. It was a tiny room. Again, the resident women were invited in,but they declined and stood in the cold passage peering into the lounge to listen.

'No one is to talk with the media,' was the direction from Jane.

After the collective had left, we had our own meeting. By now, our resident numbers had swelled to eight or more women and several kids. We agreed we needed to let all women know we were here for them. We needed to let them know they did not need a referral from an agency. They could just turn up. That was, after all, our first principle. Our second principle was that no one would be turned away. The resident women agreed with each other: the woman at the door could easily be any one of them-us. We should allow the media to announce our presence.

On Monday, when the journalist returned, I talked with him and he wrote a few words, took a photo of me hanging over the front fence and put it in the afternoon newspaper. Throughout the week, people called with more money and blanket donations and other useful stuff. It was my first lesson in the power of publicity and I learnt to use it whenever we needed help.

The newspaper article brought a flurry of new arrivals. It was heartening to see distressed women find like-minded others. Women who did not want to return to their relationships found strength in the fact there were others who felt the same. A small band of women found they had friends who understood. They were all victims of wife-bashing, women with nowhere to turn, isolated, fettered and friendless and here they were, finding a shared freedom, empathy and a sisterhood in an old derelict house.

I too found sisterhood and made many friends living in this abandoned house.

*

As time went by, not only did women come to stay at the shelter, we also had pleas from friends.

At one time, I met five young people, at their request, at the local hotel. One of the women had contacted me and asked to see me. The group were all studying at university together and were missing a fellow student. They claimed their missing friend was being assaulted and held against her will by her husband and that she wanted to go home to New Zealand. They had 'rescued' her a few days previously. The husband had caught up with them and in the ensuing all-out brawl the police were called and they took the woman to the mental hospital, with her permission and that of her husband, because she felt she would be safe there. It was common for police to agree with the husband to take the wife to the mental hospital when women lodged complaints about abuse. Complicit police found it a way of dealing with domestic violence when they were out of what they considered 'other' options.

Her friends were happy and felt they could rescue her from there later. But the husband beat them to it. A day after hospital admittance, he signed her out and took her home. He locked her in and refused her friends' requests to see her. The morning after speaking with them, I rang the hospital to verify that the wife had been admitted and then retrieved by her husband. They confirmed the story.

I met the friends again and they asked if I would go with them to her address in a small southern coastal town. I was to call, on some official pretext, and try to talk with the wife. They pointed out the house to me, I stopped in front of it in my car and they parked half a mile away to wait. I had with me a manilla folder, tucked under my arm.

I knocked on the door. As he stood in the doorway and watched me, I introduced myself without saying where I was from. 'Your wife was in hospital during the weekend and I've just come to see how she is. Could I see her?'

He was cautious and hesitated. I held out my folder with the name of his wife in big print so that he saw it and it worked. I went inside. He called his wife and as she came into the room he took her firmly by the wrist. He was taking no chances. This was tricky. How could I get around this? I asked if he would make us a pot of tea. He wavered, then let her go and went into the kitchen. I whispered to her that I had been sent by her friends and after ascertaining that she was being assaulted and that she did want to leave, I told her to get her passport and her bankbook. She tiptoed off, got them and then we high-tailed it to the waiting friends. It was that simple. All she needed was a supportive woman to help her pick up her stuff and give her the courage to leave. A few weeks later, I received a nice postcard from New Zealand.

*

Other stories emerged during those early days. The shelter also served as a haven for young single mothers. They did not all come as a direct result of a bashing but they had all been bashed and abused at some time in their short adult lives. They were in double jeopardy because, having no work and no money, they found themselves having to run from one violent accommodation to another. Welfare would be on their tails, threatening to take their child from them. There was never any suitable housing available to them. Landlords brazenly advertised, 'Children not welcome, dogs and cats okay'.

When nineteen-year-old Chantal arrived, not long after we

127

opened, she was a single mother running from welfare. They were threatening to take her eighteen-month-old toddler from her. She said that they claimed she was irresponsible, constantly moving accommodation, and she was not caring for her child. Her meagre welfare emergency payments were not enough for her to rent a place and she had been moving from friend to friend's house, picking up unsuitable 'boyfriends' from time to time. In the time she was with us, we couldn't see any problem with her parenting skills nor her morality. It was not her parenting that was a problem, it was her poverty and homelessness. Both were trifling matters according to the all-knowing, judgemental, middle-class social workers of the day.

One young single mother who turned up lost her child to welfare. When they told her that her son would be a ward of the state until he was eighteen, she tragically threw herself under a train. Her death traumatised us all. Another young mother in the same situation, after losing her little girl to welfare took an overdose at the shelter and died before the ambulance reached the hospital.

I would never advocate taking children from a violent home, from their mother, as I have heard some politicians suggest. Offer a refuge, with other women's support for immediate emergency action and, better still, arrest and charge the assailant.

One of the advantages of a women's refuge is the long- term support and advocacy that suffering women need, in order to penetrate the damaging emotional crust that keeps victims in imprisonment.

*

In the 1970s there were no welfare payments for women in desperate need for some money. Some women sought out prostitution to earn something. They were bashed and beaten by clients and pimps alike. Many such desperate women sought asylum in our women's shelter.

From early on, it became routine to talk to new arrivals around the kitchen table to ascertain in what ways we could best help them.

'Do you need money?' I quizzed one woman one night after she had settled in.

'Na,' she said, chewing at her fingernail. She did not look well.

'Are you on sickness benefits?'

'Na.'

'Are you on a pension of some kind?' I asked, thinking she might have mental issues we needed to be aware of.

'Na.'

'Are you working?'

'Yer. I'm a working girl.'

'Oh, that's nice,' I naively chatted. 'I used to be a working girl, in a canvas factory. What factory do you work in?'

By this time, the other women were giggling and the new woman looked at them, then at me. 'Is this fuckin' moll for real?'

It was my turn to raise a red face. I had never been called a moll before and coughed and spluttered as I tried to find a way out. Then I joined the women as they laughed at my naivety. This young woman was bashed and afraid of her live-in girlfriend.

I was a quick learner and did not make that mistake again. Over time, many women prostitutes (now called sex workers) would turn up from time to time at the shelter for a place of short respite. A fact often forgotten by some, is that they were also bashed, hurt and homeless, and many were supporting children.

I learnt a lot from these women about how they suffered constant moral and social discrimination. My letter to a daily newspaper spells out the legal discriminations of the day.

The letter was headed, 'Bias by men':

The recent prosecutions of women for Offences relating to Prostitution indicate a gross act of discrimination.

It is men who make prostitution illegal,

Men who enforce the law,

Men who prosecute,

Men who make judgement,

It is Men who patronise to commit the offence.
Why then, do only women get prosecuted?

*

In the first early twelve months of the women's shelter squat, many women's extreme stories filled my young naïve mind with the unimaginable. Stories of imprisonment, torture, brutality, rape, sexual servitude and child sexual abuse came my way. I had been a simple housewife and mother of three, uneducated, in a world without natural sound, catapulted onto the razor-sharp edge of learning about evil of which at times I dared not speak – who would believe me? I was alone in uncharted waters and hardly up to the bewildering unheard of challenges.

The radical collective was a side issue from the day-to-day running of the shelter. They were mostly university students or graduate teachers. They had daily commitments. I, on the other hand, ceased my factory work and committed my life full time to the shelter. I was present every day. I was personally driven by my own 'secret' life. History records many women around Australia who set up and operated women's shelters also had their own 'secret'.

I continue with a selection of stories from the women residents of the shelter of that time.

*

One cold, wet morning in late July 1974, I arrived at the shelter to find two very young teenage girls huddled on a mattress on the floor, covered in a pile of blankets. The women had let them in during the middle of the night.

They looked at me, frightened and alarmed. 'Please, please, don't dob us in to the cops,' was their first plea.

'How old are you?' I asked, as I looked more closely at them.

'I'm Julie, I'm sixteen, and she's Amanda, she's fifteen.'

'Okay. What have you done?'

'We've run away from Vaughan House. We're uncontrollable...'

Their miserable little, frightened bodies didn't look uncontrollable to me. I quickly changed to concern.

Vaughan House was a reformatory for girls. I remembered even my mother admonishing me with the threat that I would find myself in Vaughan House if I was a 'bad' girl – 'bad' euphemistically meaning girls who had been raped or sexually abused and were no longer virgins.

'Don't worry, I won't dob you in,' I said, and they told me of the ill treatment they had been subjected to and which they were trying to escape from.

'We're scared 'cause when they catch ya, ya get a cold poke – they rip yer pants off and stick their fingers up ya mick. And the nightwatchman comes around at night and shines his torch in ya face and drags ya outa bed and rapes ya. It happens to all us girls... We carn't put up with it no more. The staff know about it, but they don't do nuffin'.'

What I was hearing appalled me and now I was scared. I had no idea what I could do to help them. The welfare were responsible for their imprisonment and care; the police would obviously be looking for them. Politicians whom I had challenged would hardly sympathise. Who could I call to help the girls, what could I do, me, a squatter with no influence, no experience? I made a big mistake that was to colour my actions for the next few years.

*

As part of my involvement with a leftish community group based in Adelaide, I had met a woman who worked at Vaughan House. I truly believed that if she knew about the rapes going on at Vaughn House she would do something to help the girls. I rang her. I was oh, so wrong!

'You have to give them up,' she told me.

'But they're being raped by the nightwatchman and staff.'

'You'll have to send them back. Call the police. They'll collect them and take them back. If you don't, I will.'

'No. I won't. We have to do something to help them. I want to know that the girls will be cared for.'

I was flabbergasted. She refused to listen and said not a word about children being raped at Vaughan House. If she didn't know before, I had just told her, but she would not acknowledge it. All she kept saying was that the girls must return.

I pleaded for time. But everywhere I turned, no one wanted to know anything about girls being raped or sexually played with on a nightly basis. My heart nearly broke a few days later when she said she had called the police and I had until four p.m. Friday to call them myself or be arrested for harbouring the two runaways.

I talked with the girls. I was overwhelmed with guilt that I had caused them to be found and I offered them time to leave and run again but it was wet and cold outside and they had nowhere to go. We waited for Friday night.

'Please stay with us when the cops come,' was all they asked. 'You watch. They'ill all have taken off their identity badges and they'll get stuck into us, but if you watch, they mightn't be so bad.'

The police came and it was the most horrific display of brutal group force I have ever seen. And against two young teenage girls! Not even the Vietnam demonstrations that I had participated in evoked such a merciless onslaught. That night coloured my opinions of the police for a long while.

There were four police cars parked outside the shelter and an army marched in. I felt fear as I noticed they had no number tags identifying them. Two police stood in the passage and others stood guard at the front and back doors. The girls were sitting on the mattress where I had first seen them. The room seemed full of uniforms. I stood next to the girls as a policewoman ran in, removing her identity badge as she came.

It made me wonder what was going to happen for the police to be taking off their identity tags.

The obviously obese senior policeman said something to the girls but they did not move. He told me to stand aside and I moved two paces. He again ordered the girls to stand up. They did not move. He lunged forward with his arm to strike a blow.

I knew what a violent threat looked like and said to him, 'I'm watching you.'

'Shut your fucking face, missus, or I'll arrest you too,' he scowled.

'Please, leave them here. They'll be raped at Vaughan House,' I stuttered.

'Just keep out of this!' he stormed.

The girls were on their feet, edging away from the violent policeman, and a snatch and flurry erupted. It was like trying to catch a canary in a cage. The girls ran around in circles and the overweight policeman called others to help. The girls were caught and frogmarched up the passage between the 'guards of honour'. They were hustled away, one car for each of them.

We watched in tears as the cars drove off. We were greatly affected by the force against such young children and I was determined never to allow others – powerful men or women – to influence me ever again. I would be stronger and find a different way.

That was 1974. Clearly, 'unreported' rape and sexual abuse continued for more years at Vaughan House and I continued to hear other stories from other girls. I can only hope that 'our' girls were able to give their stories to the 2004 Royal Commission into sexual abuse in government institutions. I believe the girls should have been, maybe still need to be, compensated for their abuse, because the staff and police were told of the rape and sexual abuse and nothing was done about it.

*

Mira's story was simple and one we were able to help with. She arrived at the shelter, pregnant for the fifth time. She wanted an abortion but her husband would not allow her to have one. He tied her to the four ends of their bed and held her prisoner for an entire week. He took the other four boys to his mother's house to be looked after. While he was out at work, she escaped, collected her boys, all under the age of ten, and fled. She walked around the shopping mall during the day and slept with the boys in a secluded hideaway that night. She then telephoned Lifeline and they sent her to the shelter.

Legal abortion had just been introduced but strict qualifications applied and it was not easy to obtain. The right information and language was necessary. I was able to tap into information from the women's centre at Bloor Court and, with their help, Mira obtained her abortion. She never returned to her husband.

Forced pregnancy was a concealed, 'non-evidence-based' form of abuse imposed upon women by abusive men. It was the mid 1970s, more than ten years after the pill was introduced, and women were still being force to endure one pregnancy after the other. Before legal abortions, many women resorted to dangerous illegal procedures, either by swallowing poisonous concoctions or using crude instruments, like wire coat hangers, to remove unwanted foetuses. The women's movement were at the forefront in the fight for the right of women to have control of their own bodies. Abortions became cautiously legal with a strict time line and special conditions for the procedure to take place, and men had the right to object. Forced pregnancy is today still a 'non-evidence-based' weapon, a part of the wide spectrum of domestic violence, a powerful weapon of control in violent relationships.

I heard one woman, mother of four, say, 'He wants me to come home and have another baby.'

'Keep them barefoot and pregnant' is the old male maxim

*

A parade of young unmarried and teenage 'runaway' girls arrived at the squat shelter with similar stories of homelessness. Many were victims of sexual abuse in their family home. Single women who were beaten, raped, abused and homeless, they did not seek medical help or report to police. Reporting a rape could end up with a teenager being locked up in Vaughan House…for their protection! And older young women could have their sexual history put under a public microscope, with their reputation in tatters.

Some young mothers had babies or toddler children taken away from them by welfare – their babies and tiny children were in hot demand for fostering and welfare obliged. One young mother frequently cut deep wounds in her arms and left ugly scarring. 'I like the scars. It's something welfare can't take away from me.'

Another young girl, who had been sexually abused from a young age, kept setting fire to herself. She lay in her bed at night and set fire to her nightdress. An ambulance was called, she spent time in hospital, and when she returned I asked her why she did it.

'They can give you something for the physical pain but nothing takes away the emotional pain of what happened to me when I was a little kid.'

*

Part of my earlier life appeared at the squat shelter one morning. The front door had been left open and I was shocked to find a man walking down the passage, even more surprised when I recognised him as Dr Coats, from my hometown, Port Augusta. He had moved to Adelaide and his practice was not far from the squat.

Before I could ask him why he was there, he started at me with a brusque, 'Annette, why are you doing this? Is it really necessary for you to be squatting in this derelict house? Do women really need a women's shelter? How many women really get beaten?'

The two escapee girls' call for help still close in my mind, I turned on him. 'Who do you think you are to chastise me? How can you stand there and say that? Don't you remember poor Mrs McKenzie? She was in your hospital several times a year. You know Mr McKenzie belted her and yet no one ever charged him with assault!'

It was his turn to be shocked. No one spoke like that to almighty doctors. He turned briskly on his heels and marched out, without another word. Maybe, I thought afterwards, he had come to offer help. Had I been rash in alienating him? I regret I never saw him again, I was sad to read of his death recently; he was in his nineties and there was a long article about his many distinguished medical achievements. In a way, he was a friend. He attended my mother and my eldest daughter and my young sister were at school with his many daughters at Port Augusta.

*

Constructive community help for the shelter came from several areas and we appreciated it very much. The shelter was becoming crowded and there were always more children than women. We were delighted when a group of university students (not part of the collective) gathered together and built an inspirational adventure playground for the children. They built on the vacant block next door and the children loved it.

Other women from the community came and helped clean: they just came in, worked away and left. Their work was welcome, and we valued it.

Bashed women weren't in a state to give much effort to housework. All concentration was given to dealing with issues, and comforting distressed, wounded and grieving women.

The young members of the Lions Club and another community service group held a clean-up day and removed all the rubbish for us. Through them, we acquired a big bin which was emptied every week. Accumulated rubbish (sadly, not all donations were useful) was a constant problem and we were exceedingly grateful for their practical help.

*

Women came in at that time with sexually transmitted diseases and many had been diagnosed with thrush. As I arrived at the squat shelter one morning, I was told that there was a young woman in the bath and she had been there for a long time. I went to see if she was all right. She told me the warm water bath eased her discomfort, and she was clearly not all right. She looked dreadfully ill and was running a high temperature. I could see she was very sick and she was crying in pain. She was raw with blisters from the top of her two naked legs to her inner thighs. She told me she had thrush. She had been living on the streets after her boyfriend had bashed her and she had been sick for a long time. I knew she had more than thrush.

I rang the sexually transmitted diseases clinic on North Terrace in the city and was told to bring her in straight away. I called the women to help me get her out of the bath. We dried her, found a loose skirt and wrapped a blanket around her. Rose drove as I held her on the way to the clinic. She was admitted to hospital and returned to us some time later. She did not have thrush, but a sexual transmitted disease. She was one of those who stayed on at the shelter for the long term.

Sexual disease was a big problem for women in those days. Women were told by their doctors they had thrush and they should tell their husbands to come in for a check-up. In truth, the husband often had the serious sexually transmitted disease and had passed it on to his wife. I was told that doctors told women they had thrush so they (the doctors) would not be the ones to disclose a husband had strayed and thereby cause friction in the marriage.

*

By the end of the third month, relationships with Jane and her posse of supporters took another turn for the worse. One of them wrote a disparaging comment in the day book about one of the resident women in the shelter. Most of the comments in the book had so far been instructions for me to follow! For example, I was not to admit old women or young girls, or women who were not in a violent marriage. I only wrote in reply that I had read the comments and preferred not to respond to their instructions. It was for the women in the house to decide who they would share with. (Today's shelters need not accept women with special needs as, since those days, many types of special accommodation have been established).

One comment by a collective member in the day book was secretly read by the woman referred to, and she was rightfully distressed and angry. We held resident meetings in the lounge most days and on the day when she discovered the comment, we called an immediate second house meeting of all residents. The women were very upset that someone in a place of asylum should berate and denigrate a woman in such a way.

'Why do we have to have them here?' the woman in question said to me. 'They're not one of us. They don't do anything. And that big one [Jane], she scares me. She better not try to stick her fingers up my mick…'

We all laughed at that and the cheered-up women took to sending up the 'mafia-style macho woman'. Resident women often referred to the collective with jokes and mimicry. And the loosely stuck, tatty old radical feminist posters that refused to stick came off the walls. Any hope that the Women's Liberation Movement had of making friends with the resident women was no longer possible.

It was approaching the end of the university and school year, and volunteers numbers were dwindling.

*

We in the house had been struggling along ad hoc for a long time. The shelter was financially limping along from day to day. The utility bills were coming in and the money jar (money that was given from resident women or community support) was empty. When the electricity bill came, I called on our friendly journalist to write an article in the hope that it would bring enough donations to pay the bill. That plan backfired because a dear old gentleman pensioner went to pay the bill for us and was told that if he paid this account, he would forever be responsible for it. That made a second sensational story for our journalist. We finally did get enough cash to pay the bill.

It had become obvious we were not going to be evicted. Community Welfare (DCW) was now sending more and more women to us at the shelter and it seemed to me that it was about time the government started to think about supporting us financially. It was time to move on. A mighty change was taking place, as we decided to establish our own formal identity as a group. I consulted friends in the trade unions and one of their legal men drew up a constitution and had our group incorporated and duly registered. We set to work writing up a submission to the state government for funds to operate. It was a challenge for me and a long, interrupted process ensued. Lesbians might be lovely but they were also powerful, articulate and literate. They had resources and contacts in high places we did not.

By this time, the collective was no longer meeting at the squat shelter, but they remained active from afar, unbeknown to us. They were negotiating with DCW (who annually supplied small community grants) for funds to operate community projects. Jane reasoned that if they had funds, they would be able to employ one of the collective to take over and run the shelter.

Our group of residents submitted our own application for funding and the department was faced with a dilemma. They had two applications, one from an outside group intending to operate the shelter and one from an inside already-functioning group. We waited for the dust to settle and for an outcome.

In December 1974, six months after we squatted, Jane and her small band of loyal supporters withdrew their funding application and 'retired from the project'. The welfare department offered us, the squatters, a part-compromise. They would pay for the rental of another house if we agreed to forfeit the squat house. They would further fund us when we moved to new premises. In keeping with my objective to become 'legal', we accepted and made plans to move to 12 Churchill Road, Ovingham. This house was close by, just around the corner from our squat. It also was owned by the Highways Department under the eye of minister Geoff Virgo and so we were to became a legitimate tenant by January 1975.

It was not a good move and I was to regret it.

*

Leases for Churchill Road were signed and copies exchanged. The move took weeks and had begun slowly. We were having trouble moving into a smaller house. Where would we put all the stuff? It took time to transfer our household equipment. We walked back and forth carrying stuff. One chair at a time was carried; two women dragged heavy mattresses; tables, cupboards and bedding were all dragged one by one around the corner. Even the children helped traipse back and forth.

The house was much smaller than our squat at Torrens Road, which housed many women wanting a place of their own, and not all the women currently accommodated at the squat house would be able to go to Churchill Road. Nevertheless, I had accepted the offer from the government and we moved in.

The publicity that we were to receive state government money brought a new flood of women and before long we were to out-grow our new accommodation.

It was on one of my return trips to the squat shelter to collect more gear that we received an anonymous tip-off telling us about a group of long-standing vacant State Railway-owned cottages not far down the road at the nearby suburb of Islington. Someone from a 'high spiritual place' was watching over us!

Never ones to look a gift house in the mouth, several women piled into Rose's car and sped off to inspect. 'Great! We'll take four cottages,' Rose was quick to declare.

All hands were on deck distributing surplus equipment to the Islington cottages. We wasted no time moving four women and several children into them. Poor Rose was a regular taxi. It was the plan for women to settle in and see what happened, then send off letters to the Railways administrators offering money for rent. I reckon the women were very brave, sleeping nights in their sparsely furnished fragile dwellings unsure of what might happen to them and their children. The women were prepared to be employees of the Railways if that was required! The women's offers of rent money and becoming employees were rejected and the Islington squatting saga began.

My daily tasks were mainly for the women at Churchill Road, but I also went every day to the Islington houses to reassure the squatting women that they were not alone. They settled in but were nervous about being discovered squatting.

One day in October 1974, squatter Jeanie (an experienced squatter from Torrens Road) walked into her kitchen to find a man in working clothes standing there.

'What are you doing here? Get out of my house!' she said.

The confused man looked around the kitchen that he had expected to be empty and pulled a piece of paper from his pocket. 'This is number 246. This is my house.'

Quick as a flash and bold as brass, Jeanie replied, 'No, my house number is 246. The house next door, 248, is vacant. That must be your house. There must be some mistake. You go back and tell them, they've given you the wrong number.'

He argued a bit but Jeanie would not be put off. The poor man left, shaking his head.

The incident left the women in the other cottages nervous. They had been discovered and were expecting something to happen. Not long after, when just Rose and I were in her cottage, the expected knock came. We froze. This was it, I thought. We were in trouble. I made a quick plan. Play dumb! Rose, whose first language was Yugoslav, would confront the man and pretend she could understand only a little English. I would stand behind the door to give her encouragement. Well, I had no time to think what else to do!

'Me no spika da inglese,' attempted Rose, ridiculously slow and unconvincing.

We had the giggles.

'Your – husband – is – he – home?' The man spoke slowly, as if to an idiot.

We could hardly contain our amusement.

'Me no 'usband.' Rose sounded just as silly as she tried to convince him.

The man was not ready to give up. 'Me sell da in-sur-ance.'

That stumped us. He was no official. Get rid of him quick, I signalled to Rose.

With a burst of Yugoslav, Rose shut the door on him and collapsed in a rollicking laugh that had us both in fits. Rough tension followed by such absurdity, such was the life for squatters.

More high drama matched with high tension touched us when, a few days later, Dean Brown, Liberal member for the state seat of Davenport, visited and I got a message that the women wanted me there urgently.

I saw them talking out the front of one of the houses. Mr Brown was sympathetic to the women and I found him surprisingly easy to talk to. He promised to do all he could to help the women secure legal tenancy. A journalist arrived and the story made the front page of the *Advertiser*. Mr Brown made a flurry in parliament and the women were not bothered by anyone and in time were allowed to stay put, but not without further to-do.

Some months later, in 1975, the assistant manager for the Housing Trust rang me and suggested we go out for a coffee. We met.

'Annette, you squatting in those railway cottages has just cost the Housing Trust half our yearly budget.' He was not happy.

'What has the Housing Trust got to do with the cottages belonging to the Railways?'

'The government made us buy the whole bloody lot off the Railways. Not just yours, the whole bloody lot, at a hugely inflated price. Your fault! I'm telling you now, don't you dare ever squat in one of my houses ever again.'

I listened without sympathy, and then it was my turn to show him a truth or two. 'If you and your bloody Housing Trust would make suitable housing available for women in need, we wouldn't have to find squats. And don't tell me to apply to the Housing Trust Emergency Priority Board. We apply every week and not one of our women has ever got a house from them. What are we supposed to do?'

He was shocked and promised to look into it, but nothing substantial happened.

The problems women had with getting housing then have changed little now. Today, finding housing is still the major problem facing a woman fleeing domestic violence, especially if she has her children with her.

*

Sometime later around that time, I nominated for pre-selection as a candidate with the Labor Party and I appeared before the party executive to be examined for my credentials. At the end of the interview, executive member Geoff Virgo, who was then the minister responsible for the house that was our first squat at Ovingham, said to me, 'And tell me, Annette, if you don't get elected to the House of Parliament, will you be squatting in the House?'

4

1975–1982: Women's Stories

Before we vacated the original squat shelter, I distributed notice to all the known shelters around Australia informing them of our change of address. Our telephone number came with us.

By Christmas 1974, we were settled in the small shelter of Churchill Road. At the same time, women from around the country were on the move and within days we were in big trouble from over-crowding.

The dwelling next door to the Churchill Road shelter was a corner position with no other side neighbours. It was a large, empty shop with toilet and kitchen facilities. We surmised that the shop also belonged to the Highways Department, so several new women and children moved in, collecting bedding left at the squat shelter. It seemed like two dwellings for the price of one! No one bothered us, so the shop acted as our annexe.

January to March 1975 were hot summer months and the money promised to us from DCW did not arrive. We had no funding for equipment or food. Welfare was sending us more and more women and children. They only paid the rent of the house and we lacked other essentials; we were no better off. We had no washing machine and women were washing their children's clothes by hand in a bath. It was not an easy place to be living in. If life had been better at home, that's where women would have been.

In the winter of 1974, having no fridge at the squat was not a problem, but summer was different. We needed our grant money to be forwarded to us. And eventually it was the mothers who decided to pack up the kids, board a bus and descend on the DCW head office and enjoy their air conditioning and cool water fountains for the day. The kids ran amok enjoying themselves, darting in and out and around the many huge pot plants distributed across the open-space offices. Paper cups from the water fountain found themselves stacked into make-believe castles. And the kids had a great day.

After a few hours, a small group of women was invited into the big office to talk. The women were compelling and we left with a reassurance that we could select a refrigerator and the department would reimburse us the money.

Money! What money? Our promised money did not arrive. We waited and we waited. Then finally I arranged for a new fridge to be delivered on credit.

It took another visit to the head office of DCW from our feisty women with a reminder that we had not received our promised money, and they had to change their fiscal methods. I turned to my friendly newspaper man for support and he joined us, photographer in tow, to sit in the waiting room.

We were again invited in for talks, and after the talking was over the journalist and photographer were permitted an interview. It took a newspaper story to bring them to respond.

A man from the department came to the shelter to hand deliver a cheque to us for the fridge… Now that is service. Too bad about money to feed everyone. Only after they had seen the fridge and witnessed the invoice did they hand it over. I can understand how bureaucrats would fail to grasp how women could run an operation like we did without any money at all. They were all men and only women know how to live and survive on no money on the scale we were operating. Women are familiar with poverty, especially women victims of domestic violence. Debt is often a huge part of a household run on violence. My own house was not short of money, just short of sane management and responsibility. I often wonder how I managed the shelter so efficiently when my own home management was such a failure.

*

By this time in 1975, just one year since we were squatters, wife-bashing had been renamed to 'domestic violence' for fear, some feminists say, of offending men responsible for funding domestic violence programs.

Finance came from welfare orientation and victims were seen as 'dependent needy' recipients in need of charity. And they still are. More women were seeking to escape from it or were seeking respite. Many women came and went back and forth.

We had long discussions about domestic violence. I took notes and it became obvious to me that a pattern of abuse was emerging from the similarities of the stories. As victims, we were all the same in so many ways.

Some of us have more money than others, some of us have bigger houses than others, some of us have better education…but we all hurt, we all cry and we all hope thing will get better… In domestic violence, we are all the same.

Physical violence was not the only weapon. Verbal abuse (foul language hurled with threats and intimidation) – bullying was the invisible warfare. After many years of soul-destroying anger aimed at them, victims become ruled by fear and uncertainty and over time many souls adjust to it. It was a way of coping. Some would call it 'denial'. However, the provoking factor that caused most women to react was the sexual abuse of their children. I came to gradually realise that where there is domestic violence, there is child abuse and a huge potential for there to be child sexual abuse as well.

*

A taxi pulled up outside the shelter at Churchill Road. We were flowing over as usual. Women and children were already sleeping on mattresses all over the house; a bed was even made in the bathroom. At times like this, I regretted being persuaded to move from the squat. There, we were crowded but at least we had had enough room to move.

When the taxi pulled up, I was apprehensive. What could we offer? There was not even standing room left but I ran out to meet the vehicle. A well-dressed woman with a smart hairstyle got out with her two little girls dressed in private school uniforms. She was crying and very distressed. The taxi driver took small, expensive bags out of the boot. My heart sank. This woman was not like the others who mostly arrived with large, cheap carry-all bags, some with only plastic garbage bags. I immediately assumed she would not cope with the conditions in our shelter and wondered how the other women would cope with her. I considered asking the women who were inside whether I should invite her in, but I knew they would not refuse her so I decided not to burden them. I took it to be my responsibility. I felt obliged to consider the over-crowding. I hedged, because no woman had ever been refused accommodation before, but I felt I could not accept her. We simply had no standing space.

'I'm so sorry, I can't take you.' I was torn but I was struggling to stay focused to think of the heavily over-crowded house and the terrible conditions the resident women were enduring.

'Please, please,' she pleaded.

'Have you any money?'

'Please, we need somewhere safe,' she answered, 'and yes, I can pay.'

'No, you don't need to pay here. We just don't have any spare room. If you have money, you'd be more comfortable in a motel room.'

She looked even more distressed and she began crying. I felt terrible but I believed that I had to think of the too many women all squeezed in to the little space we had. I asked the driver to take her to a nice motel and she reluctantly got back into the taxi and left.

I still regret that decision. Domestic violence does not affect only poor and working-class women. Would I have taken her in if she had had no money? I asked myself a thousand times and I believe I would have. So does that mean I was discriminating against her because she had money? I now know that it was not only the safe accommodation she needed. It was the friendship of other women who understood. It was their companionship she needed most at that moment and money had little to do with it. I think of this woman often and regret I failed her.

*

May 1975 was bringing in the cold weather and we were still without financial help. A weekend came when we had almost no food in the house. My husband had traded his university studies for employment with the federal government and so our finances had improved. I took two women from the shelter home with me for the day and we went through my pantry. With their help, we cooked up a storm of soups and stews, bulked up with noodles. We stewed up apples and made jellies and custards. Rose, with another woman and her four kids, went to a supermarket and begged for day-old bread and they came home with heaps. In this way, we had enough food to get us through the weekend. We would worry about Monday on Monday.

On the Monday, a woman from the shelter met me at the gate. 'Quick, Annette, come with me.' She was very excited as she grabbed me by the hand and dragged me to her bedroom.

We squeezed between bags of belonging, boxes of clothing, squatting children, beds and mattresses. Finally reaching her sleeping space, she dived her hand into her pillowcase and pulled out a fistful of money rolled up in notes. My mouth fell open as she said, 'Three hundred dollars, three hundred dollars,' again and again.

'A bloke just knocked on the door and handed me the money,' she said. 'I raced and put it into my pillow and watched over it all weekend.'

I was having trouble taking it all in. It was enough that someone had just given the money like that, for the shelter, but for this woman who had no home and no money herself to hand it all to me for the shelter was incredible. She could have got on a bus with her three children and gone anywhere in Australia, who would have known? No! she handed it to me. I was overwhelmed.

There was a niggling doubt in my mind about where the money had come from. It was not unusual, at such times of our shelter's poverty, for women who were used to prostitution to go out working and come back with money or bags of food, but there were no such women in the shelter that week. So all I could do was accept the story of the money and say prayers of thanks to the generous man.

The women piled into my broken-down bomb of a car, while others pushed to get her going, and off we went to the grocer's, the butcher's and the vegie shop. The women managed to keep the shelter going for weeks on that bounty.

Despite their homelessness and poverty, honesty and integrity were the characteristics of these women at the shelter and I was proud to be able to call them my friends.

*

Resident women were slowly beginning to gain strength as they shared their stories and confronted bureaucrats and were seeing that things did not have to stay that way. They were starting to see that actions which gained public and official hearings could change things.

Winnie was older than most of the women and had a boy and girl, twin five-year-olds, from her second marriage. She told horrific stories of her bashings, and the times spent in hospital recovering. She was done with her marriage. Her interview with welfare for emergency relief money did not go well and she returned to the shelter fuming, angry and humiliated. She had had a 'slip of a man' asking her questions about her sex life, when she had last had sex, had she ever had sex in the back of the car, et cetera.

'Oh, is that all?' laughed one of the other women. 'Did he have his hand in his pocket, playing pocket billiards when he was talking to you?'

The other women guffawed and rolled around laughing at Winnie's expression. Winnie became even more indignant when they chortled, 'Welcome to the world of welfare, Winnie.'

'That's outrageous!' she raged. 'It might be all right for – you young ones – but me, at my age? Sex, in the back seat of a car? Do I look as if I'd get around in the back of a car having sex?'

The women roared with laughter again, but then sobered as we looked at the issue of the practice of welfare questioning women's sexuality. I remembered my neighbour's experience when she failed the welfare 'sex' test and was given no money. Winnie won the day with her indignation and disgust and the young women were all agreeing with her that it should not be allowed to happen.

Winnie was the daughter of a miner, a countrywoman from Broken Hill. She vowed we should do something about it and turned to me. 'Well, Annette, what are you going to do about it?'

'Me?' I squeaked. 'What are *you* going to do about it?'

'United we stand, divided we fall!' she declared.

'OK, OK, what are we *all* going to do about it?'

We decided to go en masse to the head office again and complain.

Next day, eight women accompanied Winnie and me as we led our little band of sisters to present our complaint to one of the senior bureaucrat at the main DCW office.

'Oh, not that complaint again,' he said as I stared at him aghast. 'We've been hearing about that one for years.'

'So you know about these questions to women about their sex lives?' I asked in more of an accusation.

'Oh yes. That's been department policy for years.'

'Why?'

'Well, we have to establish who the father of the child is.'

'Have you heard of birth certificates?'

We exchanged increasingly heated words but the women were not satisfied with his answers and demanded that the practice be stopped forthwith.

He fumbled with his words. 'You must understand…' he tried.

Understand? Was he kidding? These abused and now domestically liberated women understood only too well. They had been abused by their husbands and now had to accept abuse from departmental sleazes. They were having no more of that. The women became raucous and crude and began throwing questions at him about his sex life. He was clearly uncomfortable. The women lacked refinement and they did not beat about the bush. They were bawdy, strong women, solid in their new-found strength and sisterhood. As his face grew redder and redder, the sisterhood grew more powerful.

He stuttered that he would investigate a change in departmental policy and their answer to that was, 'Yer, and you can tell 'em to stop playin' pocket billiards when they talk to us…or we'll be back.'

This venture into the welfare office with complaints about the treatment of women was the first of many group engagements with welfare to complain about departmental attitude to women. We began to see minor changes as women began to assert themselves and demand better. We were a band of shameless hussies and we sang the song written by Jenny Pausacker in the early 1970s. ('Hussy' is an old English word for housewife.)

> Chorus: 'We're shameless hussies and we don't give a damn
> We're loud and raucous and
> We're fighting for our rights
> And our sex and for fun, and we're strong'
> Were shameless hussies and we curse and we swear
> We will be free, beware to those who disagree
> Come and sing, come and fight
> And we will win!

*

Our small house and even the annexe in the Churchill Road shelter were full. There were so many women we could have fielded two football teams. Many of the women were steamed up with indignation about their lot as women and were ready for more assertive action.

Then Helen arrived for the second time. The shelter women had been gaining confidence by asserting themselves in various fields and Helen's case called for some practical intervention.

'You'd better come and get this woman out of my taxi,' called the taxi driver.

I ran out and saw Helen. She had not long been a resident in the Churchill Road shelter and had decided to return to her husband a couple of weeks earlier. I thought she might have returned home because of the crowded conditions, as I suspected many women might have. She was in such pain that she could not even ease herself out of the taxi. She needed to be in hospital. I ran back into the house and told the women to get Rose to pick me up from the hospital.

I got in the taxi with Helen and the hospital staff helped her get out. Neither of us had any money to pay the fare but the driver asked for none. He just said goodbye and drove off. I met many generous taxi drivers delivering women to the shelter in those days. Helen was admitted and I left her in their care. Rose was waiting for me and we returned to the shelter.

Rose was one of the squatters in the railway cottages and was a constant worker and friend for the shelter. Her clapped-out little car was always on call, and she was one of the many reliable unsung women heroes, who were always willing to lend a hand.

Next morning, I went back to see Helen. She had broken bones in her back but she would heal.

She muttered, 'You remember, Annette, the last time I was in the shelter? I asked you to help me and some of the women to come home with me and give him a good bashing and you said, "No, we couldn't do that." I wish we had gone off and done it. Then I might not be like this now.'

I returned to the shelter sunk in my feeling of guilt. Violence is not my calling and I had refused to go with her; nor would I hear of other women from the shelter taking to violence. I felt guilty because I wavered in courage to help her confront her husband and now she had broken bones in her back.

I told the women what Helen had said.

'Right! That's it!' said one woman, ready for some justice 'Let's do it.'

A round table conference was held and the women hatched a ridiculous plan.

'No, we can't do that!' I said, still unsure about it.

'OK, then what about this?'

'No, not that either.'

'Look, Annette. Are you with us or against us? Remember, united we stand, divided we fall.'

'Oh, all right.' I gave in. 'So what are we doing?'

Among the next-door shop residents were two mothers with several children who had made their way from Perth and whose 'careers' in their previous lives were mistresses, specialising in sex fantasies and domination. So they said. They were a hoot. One was older than the other and they had the house in roars of laughter when they recounted incidents from their careers. I hope they will forgive me for saying this, but they were the most unlikely-looking pair I could have imagined to be performing in this way. They were more comedians than sex fantasists.

But the plan was hatched. Winnie and other women would stay at home to care for the children while the rest of us watched as the two experienced ones made their preparations to lead the way. They painted their faces and dressed themselves in the most ridiculous non-sexy outfits. They looked more like clowns. The younger one was very pregnant and her belly hung out over her short shorts. I suggested that she shouldn't really go on this mission in her condition.

'Nar,' she said, picking up a huge rolling pin and tapping it across her palm. 'These guys love a big belly.'

Oh well, what would I know!

Then they collected together their 'toys', rolling ropes into lassos and cracking home-made whips and adding a pillowcase for a blindfold. We couldn't contain our hysterical, ribald mirth as we watched them gather their tools of trade. Then it was down to business. We tried not to laugh out loud as we watched them rehearse. This was serious business.

The real action began late that night, Rose drove five or six of us in her little car to the house where Helen lived. A group of other women followed in another car. The house was in darkness and the two fancy-dressed women got out of our car. They knocked on the front door. It opened and there he stood, tall and glorious in his shabby pyjamas.

'We're here to give you a good time,' one woman crooned as the rest of us stood back out of sight in the shadowy branches of nearby bushes.

He was delighted and beckoned the two mistresses inside and they put a pillowcase over his head and then beckoned us all to sneak in quietly. The women all joined in. The plan was to get him trussed up and then...

He was a tall man and they had trouble getting the rope around his neck, but he obliged, reaching up his hands and tucking it where they wanted round his neck. Truly, he helped tie himself up! The end of the rope dangled from his neck and he twirled his body so the rope coiled round like a python and he did what the women wanted. He seemed to know the routine. Then someone yanked the rope and, with a kick to his legs from another woman, brought him to the floor, where they all gave him a kicking saying, 'This is for Helen.'

Suddenly he realised why they were there. He just lay on the floor like log of rolled corned beef awaiting his fate.

'Don't hurt the kid, don't hurt the kid,' he whined.

We were stunned. What kid? There was no child in this house.

A woman raced around the house in search. 'There's a kid in his bed,' she cried and, in a flash, she pulled the man's pyjama pants down and grabbed his penis, 'Ooh yuk, he's been fucking the kid. His dick is all slimy and sticky.'

The women gasped.

I went to look and saw a naked boy about six years old in the double bed.

I spoke to him, trying to coax him out. 'Are you all right? Where's your mother? Who are you?' but he was very frightened of me and burrowed himself under the blankets. I paused, wondering what to do, and decided I was causing him more distress, so I returned to the women.

'Right, let's go,' I said. I knew we had to leave. We were frightening the child and we had made our point. I would deal with the matter of the child later. There was also a need to get away quick as I had organised a tip-off, naming the address for a newspaper journalist to find a tied-up naked man with a sign 'wife-basher' around his neck. He could be here any minute.

Our drivers backed up and I opened the back door of Rose's car. Without warning, a really huge, bloody great big hairy dog appeared from nowhere and jumped into the back seat. The dog was so big and the car so small that he took up the whole back seat.

'Quick, get in, get in,' shouted anxious Rose.

'Can't. Got a dog in the back seat!'

'Well, get the bugger out.'

'Can't, the bugger won't move.'

We pushed and pulled and he wouldn't budge. What sort of a quick getaway was this?

We were making a big racket, laughing and calling out and the dog just sat there panting, his sloppy tongue hanging out.

'Oh no, not you too,' said the woman in fancy dress and everyone laughed.

I was expecting people to come out of the next-door houses to see what the noise was about and we would be sprung, so three of us just piled in on top of the dog. Rose slowly eased from the kerb with us squeezed in the back, a hairy tail wagging in our faces. Everyone was laughing fit to burst, but all I could think of was the consequences. It would be bad enough being had up for assault and sexual harassment, but dognapping as well? And what to do about the child?

It was past midnight. I saw a telephone box and got Rose to stop the car so I could make an anonymous call to the police. When the car door opened, the dog just struggled out and bounded off. He had only wanted a car ride. I had insufficient coins and my call did not get through.

Next morning, I rang the journalist and he said he went to the address but it was all dark and quiet and there was no naked man in the lawn. I was relieved. Later, I got a phone call from the man we assaulted. He was actually thanking me for what we did. I tried denying it was us, and then wondered what he was really thanking us for. Then it hit me he might have been thanking me for doing nothing about the child. I was repulsed and visited Helen in hospital. I told her about the child in her husband's bed. She shocked me when she said that the boy was his nephew; she seemed to know what was going on. She said, reluctantly, she would do something about it, but we did not hear from her again after she had regained her health.

*

However, there was another serious and lasting problem for many bashed women over which we were unable to have any influence. Bashed, isolated and desperate women went to their doctors.

Raelene explains the issue in simple terms:

I went to the doctor some years ago. I had a black eye and other bruises, and I cried and cried as I tried to tell him about my situation. I told him I got the bruise on my face because my husband bashed me. Mmy eye was so swollen I couldn't see from it. The doctor didn't look at me the whole time I was crying. He said nothing and just gave me a prescription for Valium – and I've been on them ever since.

Myriad women consulted doctors when they were damaged and

suffering trauma. They were prescribed addictive drugs and remained on them for many years. I have met women today, no longer living with their abuser, but still being prescribed and taking addictive drugs.

'I can't manage being without them,' a long-term user of doctor-prescribed addictive drugs, recently told me.

*

Following the end of 1974 and into 1975, many new shelters were being established around the country and we were all beginning to contact each other. Several interstate conferences were held and we joined in coalitions, with regular contact. Because of tireless efforts and campaigning from the women at Elsie Women's Refuge (the first refuge in Australia) in Sydney, and other associated refuges, together with help from women members of the federal government, federal funding was announced.

In June 1975, I received a telegram from the federal government, which now had Whitlam at the helm, saying they would be allocating substantial ongoing funding to eleven women's shelters and refuges around Australia and we were one of them. The WEL was also a beneficiary of the block of funding and set up another shelter in North Adelaide. With the promise of this funding, the SA Housing Trust purchased a nice house for the WEL group and a much bigger house for us that I had found on Prospect Road, Prospect. Because the Housing Trust agreed to make some structural alterations to suit our needs, it would be a while before we could move in. At the Churchill Road shelter, we were still struggling along, always overflowing.

*

It was October 1975, holiday time for schoolchildren, when two teenage girls were found hiding among the bushes in the backyard of the Churchill Road shelter. The women brought them inside and cared for them over the weekend, but they ran away on Monday morning before I arrived. I left instructions to encourage the girls to stay if they should come back. The girls returned, and they were there on Tuesday morning when I arrived.

Fear, real fear, has an aura that needs no words from the victim. It radiates its own language. I could see the aura of fear around the girls. They were undersized for their age, skinny and malnourished. Their clothes hung from their tiny bodies and they were constantly chewing their fingernails, right down to the raw skin at their fingertips. They were a pitiful sight.

'You have to talk to them right now,' the women told me. 'There's something wrong, really wrong, here.'

'What do you mean?' I asked.

'They're in serious trouble,' one woman said.

'How do you know?'

'We just know! Talk to them now.'

When I saw the girls, I knew them. They were sisters. Jenny was fifteen years old and Anne was thirteen. They were friends of my youngest daughter. They had brought no change of clothing and it was clear things were not right with them.

The sisters were huddled close together on a mattress on the floor. I asked them to come into the next room, where we could sit on a bed. There were three beds in this tiny room and floor space for a mattress that was now stored leaning up the wall; there was no room for any other furniture. They walked in cautiously and sat opposite me on a bed piled with stored bedding. They dangled their swinging feet off the floor, twisted their hair between their fingers and chewed their fingernails. They did not raise their gaze off the floor. They were giggling nervously and forced their bony little fists into their mouths.

I just looked at them. Nothing was said and I was unsure how to proceed. It bothered me that they would say nothing at all when I asked them why they could not go home. They were too young to be here on their own. They did not answer but exchanged looks between themselves. They kept darting side glances at each other. Who was going to speak? Who was going to tell?

I knew the girls had two older sisters. One was nineteen and the other was twenty. There was an older brother, eighteen years old, and a younger sister of nine.

We sat in silence, then I started gently coaxing, asking gentle questions.

After a while, one of them said, 'Harry' – the name of their older brother.

The other said quietly, 'Dad…'

Two males in one family told me a lot.

It was a very painful meeting. All I could do was sit and wait and gently coax them to continue. One word at a time with intervening nervous giggles, then a few more words. It took all my concentration to try to piece the story together. Because the girls were so distressed, I swallowed my need to know why they were at the shelter. For the moment, it seemed obvious to me there was serious family mischief and I simply reassured them they were safe here and I and the women would protect them and sort something out.

Looking back as I write this, I can't help but bring up my memories of telling those girls in all sincerity that they were safe with me. With this memory comes shame and guilt. I now know that while I was saying those words to the girls, my own children were suffering and living in fear in their own home. I still cannot understand why I was so blind to that. Like so many women, I believed that I was the one my husband was set against. I thought my children were safe. I was wrong, I was, oh so wrong. All children living with domestic violence are unsafe. They hear, they see, they feel, they cry, they suffer, they know, they fear. They are traumatised, the same as their mothers.

'No, he wouldn'ot hurt the children,' I had said. I did not see the obvious. I did not say to my own children, 'I'll protect you. You're safe with me,' and all that time they were not safe and I was not protecting them.

It took several days to find out from the sisters what they were afraid of. I initially agreed with them not to call the police, but when they had finished their tale, I had no option.

The sisters were more comfortable talking to the women around the kitchen table and after a few days they calmed down. Days later, they spoke to me in intense, short, sharp sentences. Parents away. Brother looking after them. Belts them. Sex with them. Father has sex with them, Father makes them 'practise' sex with objects while father watches. Ran away from him. Dad abusing them. Weekend bowling trips – forced to have sex with him and his mates. Dad bashed mother. Father took photos of girls in forced sexual acts with each other. The family had a big Alsatian dog. The story grew worse and worse. There was pornography, sexual servitude, violence, rape, torture. They were in terror for their nine-year-old sister. She was the age when he 'started' with them.

I had to tell the girls the only way they could help their sister was to notify the police and the welfare. Even as I said that, I held out little hope. The police had so often dismissed women's stories; would they believe children? I doubted it. But something had to be done and I could not dismiss the magnitude of the situation. They were in a panic; they might be forced to go back. But not if I could help it! I assured them I would deal with that if it looked like happening.

I rang the police and welfare. There was no response after a few days. A woman I knew who volunteered at Lifeline helped me get through, and the police took notice. The welfare came and talked with the girls and the police took lengthy statements from them at the police station. They said they believed the girls and that their individual stories matched. I was relieved. The police believed they had enough evidence to prosecute.

We were delighted the girls were believed and prosecution was expected. But now we were to worry what would become of Jenny and Anne. They were under threat from the family's older sibling and there were failed attempts to abduct the sisters from the Churchill Road shelter. They did not venture outdoors and we kept a very close eye on them. But not close enough.

One day, a social worker from DCW came for the sisters to take them for interviews. They did not return them to the shelter, instead taking to Vaughan House.

I was furious. Welfare was placing them into the hands of known paedophiles. I had alerted them to that in 1974.

The police arrived in force with welfare and told me that Jenny and Anne had escaped from Vaughan House. I smiled to myself. 'Clever little girls. They'll be back.'

'No, they're not here,' I told them.

'If they come here, you will let us know, won't you?'

I was angry. 'How come you guys are chasing around after two innocent children to lock them up – and yet you're allowing a paedophile to roam free. Do you guys really think that if a cunning paedophile father couldn't keep them locked up in his prison, you blokes could keep them locked up in yours?'

The welfare and police made several trips to the Churchill Road shelter searching for Jenny and Ann. But I didn't need to get myself in a stew! The sisters escaped Vaughan House and managed to get back to the shelter that night under the cover of darkness. Some of the women in the house had been victims of child sexual abuse and had themselves been locked up as teenagers. That was how they knew there was something really wrong. They were overjoyed to see the sisters returned.

I was having none of the fiasco of the earlier months in 1974 at the squat house with the runaway Vaughan House girls. This time, I vowed Jenny and Anne would be protected no matter what.

Of course, the police and welfare were back in no time at all.

'They're not here,' I said. I had taken the precaution of placing them in the shop next door under the protection of street smart women.

'You will tell us if they come here, won't you?'

'Of course I will, officers.'

'They're runaways and you'll be charged with harbouring escapees if you don'ot hand them over.'

I had heard this line of threat before. 'Yes, yes, I'm aware of that!'

How could this be? An abusive, paedophile father was living free and able to carry on while two innocent young teenage girls were wanted, hunted like criminals, and were being pursued to be dragged back to institutional imprisonment. It was disgraceful! What were men doing?

The shelter was under siege with constant police and welfare visits. A welfare man came to the shelter and read me the riot act, saying that if the girls were to appear, I had to send them back immediately to Vaughan House. I laughed in his face and said I would never do that and would go to prison myself if that was the alternative. I asked him why the girls could not be placed in a nice family home with good care.

He gloated when he explained that girls 'like them' could not possibly be placed in 'a nice family home'.

I saw red! 'Girls like that!' I almost spat at him. How dare he! I stared him down in fury but he persisted in telling me that girls 'like them' would undoubtedly accuse the man of the 'nice family' of inappropriate conduct.

I was fuming mad by that time. 'Well, I'm not going to hand them over to you or anyone else, so you can just piss off out of here.' Not my usual language, but I was defiant and red mad. I was looking for the shock element. I stormed at his stunned face and held my head high as he turned and left, with dire warnings about consequences for me.

Welfare took the case for guardianship of Jenny and Ann to the Children's Court. It was scheduled for a couple of weeks on. I intended to be there to present a case for us to have interim custody until something better could be provided for them. Meanwhile, the police kept up regular visits and our game of cat and mouse played on. Police and welfare visits waned and I became worried we could be caught by a surprise strategic visit.

One day, I suggested to the girls that I ring the police and tell them they had come back to the shelter, rather than wait in constant suspense for a surprise visits. Then, as the police dispatched a car, I asked Rose to take the girls for a drive, anywhere, just away for the day – I didn't need to know where. When the police came and searched the shelter, they found no girls.

'I told the girls you were coming,' I said, 'and they took off. I have no idea where they might have gone.'

'Hmm. Call us if they come back,' was the curt request, and my answer was a meek 'Of course, I will, officer.'

This farcical scenario played out two or three more times and took us up to the court hearing. Fortunately, the magistrate was a person of common sense and I was awarded interim custody of Jenny and Ann.

I took the girls home with me for several days before returning them to the shelter. My own husband complained when they arrived to stay, saying that they would most likely falsely accuse him as a male of being a sexual predator. What? Oh no, not you too, I thought.

*

My domestic situation did not change much throughout the time I was involved with women's shelters. The violence was sporadic and unabated. I was not bashed as often as I might have been had I stayed in the home. At the first indication a bashing could happen, I was out the door, running and hiding for my life. Strangely enough, I never thought to stay at the shelter myself, because the shelter was always so full and I didn't want to take up the space another woman might need. Yet there were too many of my hours spent at the shelter, early mornings and late nights, too many hours that I did not spend with my own children. They were left in Mack's care far too often and far too long. They paid a heavy price for my absence and blindness.

Somewhere around that time, Mack added new maxims to his expanding repertoire. 'You couldn't survive without me. You'are nothing without me. I made you what you are today.'

My predicament did not escape the women in the house. One day,

I took off my cardigan and forgot I had knuckleprint bruises on my arm.

The all-seeing women challenged me. 'What happened here, Annette?' someone said.

I slid away and said nothing.

Next thing, women bailed me up. 'How dare you come here and not tell us when you've been bashed. We take you into our confidence and we tell you our story.'

I mumbled something and felt humiliated by my inability to tell. But I thought about what the women said to me and did seek comfort from shelter women shortly after.

I remember one night, after a torrent of abuse, I ran from the house and went to the home of, Pamela one of the women squatting at Islington. After a long tearful night of talking and her consoling me, I slept on her lounge. Late into the night, I was woken up by the sound of a car pulling into the driveway and two noisy men got out. I went to the window and I was shocked to see Mack and a man I did not know. They banged on the front door. Pamela answered and told them to go away.

'I'm sorry to tell you, Annette, but Mack has been visiting women down here, and there are others too. They pissed him off, but the women were too concerned for you to tell you.'

Violent men have secret lives; it's all part of them spreading their influence afar.

*

By the end of 1975, with future funding assured and a renovated house, we moved to our final resting place, Prospect Road, Prospect.

With money in the bank for the first time ever, our move at the beginning of 1976 was much easier than all the others and we set about installing good equipment under our grant allocation for equipment – new pots and pans, a new fridge and freezer and other essentials as we needed them. Number one was a super-duper commercial laundry: no more washing sheets and dirty nappies in the bathtub.

Sydney's Elsie Women's Refuge set the trend by giving their shelter a name and we followed suit and called the new house Naomi Women's Shelter. We were now fully government-funded and our future was financially secure.

But the women's stories of domestic violence continued to be told.

The two sisters Jenny and Ann came with us to Prospect and stayed, protected at Naomi Women's Shelter, waiting for their father to be prosecuted.

*

Despite our good fortune and new-found wealth, some things did not change. Safe, ongoing appropriate housing was still the biggest issue for women wanting to leave violent relationships and so a group of women at the Churchill Road shelter and the annexe, considering it mad to leave a house vacant when so many women were in dire need, decided not to move with us to Prospect, and stayed on. I terminated our lease with the Highways Department and paid the week's rent for the moving week. The remaining women said they would negotiate their rent with the department but they didn't and Churchill Road remained a squat. Later, that brought trouble to my door yet again – but it was later resolved. The Highways Department accepted that we had properly terminated our agreement and their issue was with the squatting women and children. They were not troubled and later secured better public housing.

With the growing positive government attitude towards shelters, more opened and we were in contact with many of them. We all had different ideas about how a shelter should be run. Some felt the address should be kept secret but I, with the resident women, held the view that a boldly painted sign out the front in full view would tell women where we were and would allow any woman, without referral, to knock on our door at any time, day or night, and be welcomed. And what man would come knocking bringing trouble to our door when he could be seen in full view from the main road? It would blow his cover and expose him as a wife-basher.

But abusive men did come knocking on the door and I felt sorry for some of them.

'What's going on?' one man asked me. He came looking for his wife and I could not tell him if she was with us or not.

'It's all right for her, she has got you people, but us blokes, we have no one to talk to. I went to welfare but they said they were helping women and children, they couldn't talk to me.'

I later pondered this man's concerns and realised it was pointless in the overall scheme for us to be helping women, only to leave blokes with no input to understanding what was happening and free to continue their violence with the next woman and any children they took up relations with.

*

There was an incident with two resident children.

'Look, there's my daddy,' said a small child, while on an outing with our childcare worker. The child pointed out a man standing at a set of traffic lights.

'That's not your daddy, that's my daddy,' said a slightly older child.

The conversation carried on, and back at the shelter the two boys kept talking. The mothers got involved and, after much comparing, discovered both children were right. The abusive man left one relationship and had more children in another.

It was this realisation that caused me to begin talking to one or two men in our office. But it was not long before resident women objected and I stopped counselling men at the shelter. But I did set up meetings in a distant borrowed office.

I found there were men who could respond and benefit from

appropriate counselling. At the time, my skills were minimal and I found men needed more than I could offer. And the women still objected: they thought I was being disloyal to them. I agreed my actions could be seen as undermining the plight of abused women and I stopped my attempts to help men see the error of their ways. A small number of women were appreciative of the opportunity to have someone talk to their husbands and put their concerns to them – not all women wanted to end their relationship;, they just wanted the violence to stop and to be treated better. I was probably also locked in this category at the time.

I still maintain, if we are to make any headway into reducing domestic violence, abusers must be given the opportunity of quality rehabilitation, as most of them come from an abusive home and have never been given the chance to recover. Others should be prosecuted like any other offenders.

*

I did continue to offer help to men who were victims of abuse and my actions were sparked by an incident after we spent the day delivering furniture to a newly settled woman and her children.

It was a very hot forty-degree day when I hired a trailer. Glenda, Lily and I went to our favourite second-hand shop for furniture. We piled the trailer high with beds, wardrobes, a fridge and a kitchen table. I spied four fantastic cane antique commode chairs complete with ceramic potty, at a dollar a chair, and couldn't resist them; they would be great for dining chairs. I loved old commode chairs and had a fabulous collection of them. I gave one to my niece for her birthday; she thought I was weird!

Driving north on Prospect Road heading for Kilburn, one of my prize commodes fell off the trailer. The ceramic potty rolled down the road and I was worried it would be damaged. Then a second chair fell and I was beside myself with concern.

I pulled up quick and pushed Lilly out of the car. 'Quick, Lily, get out and rescue the commodes before someone runs over and smashes them.'

I parked a little further down, where it was safe, and ran back to Lily. I could hardly believe my eyes. There was Lily sitting on one of the commodes with her feet up on the other one gently puffing on a cigarette. Cars slowed and drove around her, the drivers waved and tooted good-humouredly at her. You don't often see a woman sitting on two commode chairs in the middle of a main road to the city. She waved back with a friendly air. Despite her pit stop, she saved the day – my precious commodes were safe.

We managed to deliver the furniture and helped the resident to set up her house. The kids all loved the big armchair commodes around the table, but mother was not so sure.

'A dollar each – you'll love them,' I said.

The day was over and we were hot, dirty and exhausted. Moving house was all in a hard day's shelter work.

'I need a beer,' said Lily.

There were not many people in the front bar and we settled down to talk of the day's events.

Blokes were jeering, making fun of us in the front bar. 'What these Sheilas doing in 'ere? You Sheilas got balls or somefin'?'

Women were expected to be ladylike and sit in the ladies lounge, but lounge prices were higher than the front bar and that was discrimination, we reckoned.

We managed to ignore them until one big burly bloke said, 'Look at that piss weak wimp,' meaning the man sitting around the corner from him. 'He lets his wife beat him up. She'll be here soon. Give him a right bashing. Weak bastard. He lets her get away with it.'

We glared at the big man. Then we took notice of the poor man getting berated. He hung his head and appeared depressed. On and on went the abusive man until Lily could stand it no longer.

She looked at me with a challenge in her eye. 'What do you ya reckon?'

We got off our stools, walked up and spoke to the man under attack. He was almost in tears. We offered words of comfort to him as best we could.

Lily, a tall, strong, handsome-looking woman, stepped closer to the loudmouth man and said in a loud brusque tone, 'Leave him alone, you big bully.' (Or words to that effect.)

He turned to look at Lily, a long up and down sort of look, and in a smug put-down sort of way said, 'Gee,s luv, I'd like to get into your knickers.'

Lily, always ready with a quick retort, slowly took a big draw of her cigarette, gave him the same slow up and down look and said, 'Why, mate? Did you crap in yours?'

The three obnoxious men just laughed but seeing that poor dejected man made us think about how men treat other men who are abused. Men can be victims of domestic violence and services need to be available for them.

*

A short time after we had settled into Naomi, one obnoxious man did come knocking. I spoke with him on the front veranda. He was asking about a resident and put on a right performance of yelling and screaming demanding to speak with 'his woman'. He would not be pacified and his temper was rising. He was threatening and becoming very agitated. It was frightening when he began making serious threats.

Finally, I said, 'If you don't leave…' and he butted in, 'Yer, yer, I know. You'll call the cops.' And he continued to make nasty threats.

'No, no, I won't call the police, I'll call a doctor and have you certified to a mental institution. You must be mad; no sane man would carry on like you.'

He stopped in his tracks, stunned and then ran from the shelter.

'Well, that worked well,' I thought!

A few days later, there were two detectives on the front veranda asking about the same woman. I declined to give them any information about her.

'Do you know a man called Josef?' one asked.

'That little pipsqueak? Yes, he was here a couple of days ago. I threw him off the veranda.'

'You what?' The detectives turned red.

I repeated what I'd done and said to the mad man.

'He's a very dangerous man. No one should approach him. We want him because we believe he stabbed a man to death a few days ago. And…you threw him out? He said he was with the missus the whole night. We just want to verify his whereabouts.'

'Well,! I can tell you she wasn't with him. She's afraid of him and she was here all night. I myself was here late and other women can tell you she hasn'ot left the shelter since she arrived.'

'Thank you very much,' they said, shaking their heads as they left.

*

At the Naomi Women's Shelter we were able, with our first quarterly advance payment, to set up a super-duper laundry with two industrial washing machines and a huge gas-fired industrial clothes dryer. We got lots of new bedlinen and set up a wonderful kitchen. Women who left the shelter or even just came to visit were invited to come back and use the laundry. Many women who were trying to set themselves up in homes were often unable to afford things like washing machines.

With our new-found wealth, we were able to afford paid staff, but soon found that those employed from outside did not understand domestic violence unless they had been there themselves, and so we found it best to offer staff wages to ex-residents who had been contributing to the running of the shelter before we had money.

The publicity around our pending new facility gave more and more abused women the possibility of considering other options and also gave them choices. Before we knew it, we were bubbling along with more women and children than ever. Our money worries were over and we had no need to encourage donations. We appointed an accountant to take care of the book-keeping and he gave strict instructions to keep receipts and to bank any donations. He produced quarterly audits for the government departments that dealt with grant money and they would then forward to us the next three-month grant.

Small cash donations continued to be dealt with in-house by the women. There was always some woman needing something not included in our government allocation – an airplane ticket to flee interstate, help with their electricity bill, a week's rent to tide them over. These payments, if they were spent from government grant money, would be called 'misappropriation of government money', so we only used our privately donated money for extras. Nevertheless, I experienced this accusation some time later.

Many kind people knocked on our door and handed money to women. We were able to thank them, but others sent money anonymously. Each year a cheque arrived, and only years later did I find out the story behind the generous gift. Two adult sisters grew up with domestic violence and were desperate to rescue their ageing mother while she was still young enough to enjoy her life. The sisters bought her a small flat, but tragically their mother died before she could move in. The sisters rented out the flat and at the end every year they sent Naomi Women's Shelter their small profit, in memory of their mother. We invested it in activities and seaside holidays for the children. I think of the sisters and their mother whenever I bring out the photos of happy children playing on the beach.

We always had more children than women in the house and we were to apply to the federal Office of Child Care for grant money to provide special care for the children. A large shed was built at the back of the house and we employed a woman who was a trained schoolteacher. She was wonderful and the children loved her.

A bigger house meant more women, and children. Race, ethnic

background and language were no problem. Women were women, and all lived together in harmony and compassion.

*

Many migrant women came to the shelter, and for a while we had an influx of Asian women. Australian men were sourcing Asian brides' and treated them like slaves. We heard appalling stories of slavery and prostitution forced upon them. Alone, and with little English as they were, we were unable to be of much help to them. They moved on quickly but more kept coming.

Greek and Italian women who spoke little English found their way to the shelter and I saw a different side to violence. Maria came without her three-year-old little girl and somehow, through difficult communication, we discovered that she and her child had been held prisoner by her husband and guarded by her mother-in-law in his mother's home. The woman escaped, but was forced to leave her child behind under the heavy guard of her mother-in-law. She begged me to drive her to help her rescue her little girl.

We drove up an unsealed dusty road, past long rows of cabbages, cauliflowers and other vegetable gardens, when she suddenly called 'Stop. Stop.'

The child was in the front garden of a house.

Maria bounded from the car, grabbed the pretty little girl and quickly jumped back in. 'Go. Go,' she yelled.

I drove fast up the dirt track spitting back sand and was horrified when the track came to an end. I had no choice but to turn round and pass the house again. I could see a man standing in the middle of the track pointing a rifle at us and I considered the options – there weren't many. I had no path or bush to drive further forward. I turned the car round and stopped to look further ahead and think. If I drove at him, would he jump aside? Would he fire at us? Should we hand the child back?

'What do you want to do?' I asked Maria.

'Go. Go,' she said.

She put the child on the floor and I put my foot flat to the floor and headed straight at him. He jumped out of the way. 'Phew,' I thought as we tore past him in a swirl of sand and dust, but then I heard the gun go off, zing! and then a second time. I saw him in the rear-view mirror aiming the rifle and heard the bullet whizz past the window.... !

We got back to the shelter. While I was very shaken, Maria was elated to have her child and seamed undisturbed by the ordeal. I had never been shot at before, but for Maria it was a constant threat – and now she was free.

A little while later, a migrant women's shelter was established.

*

Many Indigenous women came to the shelter. They always came with more children than non-Aboriginal women. Mostly, their houses were overcrowded with visiting country relatives and the abused women would not leave the children when there was violence brewing.

One woman was Lorna. A male relative came to her house demanding money from her. She refused and was attacked and threatened with further assault. The man threatened to come back with the father of one of the children she was keeping safe. Lorna fled with the children to the safety of the shelter.

Generally, Aboriginal women also had more serious injuries. It was often difficult for them to escape. They were less likely to be able to call taxis. They had no money and did not own a vehicle, or have immediate access to a phone, and they did not seek medical help. Very few called for police assistance. They had complex problems and were divided as a community on the question of seeking police help. Many women felt extreme pressure to avoid police and legal intervention, as their history was filled with discrimination.

Aboriginal women with very different cultural diversities from non-Aboriginal women considered they needed a shelter specifically for them. I shared their idea that they should have their own shelter, to be run by Aboriginal women. I took Lorna and another Aboriginal woman to meetings with politicians and bureaucrats to help with submissions for considerations. They were not received well.

A senior bureaucrat was embarrassed when I introduced Lorna to him with stories of the specific difficulties Aboriginal women faced in comparison to non-Aboriginal women. Their men were more violent, more often, the women more damaged, they had more children, had cultural differences, and racial concerns that they felt the need to support their men and were unable to dob them in. Police were the enemy of Aboriginal people, and any consultation with police caused great friction within their community.

The bureaucrat was embarrassed by my direct approach and replied with apologies. 'I apologise for Annette and what she said about your husbands.'

Lorna was amused. 'You no need apologise for Mizz Annette. You listen to her, she tell you good.'

We left the multistorey building and were laughing at the agitation of the poor bureaucrat – he was clearly uncomfortable discussing issues which affected Aboriginal women.

'Why did you speak to him like that?' I asked her – Lorna spoke perfect English.

'Silly white fella – stupid bugger,' she continued mockingly as we went on our way. It was her way to counter what she felt was his condescending behaviour and not listening to their concerns. She wanted to treat him like he was a 'goose'.

The women were not put off. They had been rebuffed before. They dealt with the daily challenges with humour and were a ball of fun. Lorna eventually lost her private rental and got an Aboriginal funded house. The state Housing Trust had different sections and received 'specific Government funding. For specific "welfare" groups'. This section was administrated by Aboriginal people within the Housing Trust. The houses were purchased by the Housing Trust and scattered around the state.

Lorna invited me to visit her.

'I don't know where you live,' I said.

'You know Roberts Street?'

'Yes! I know the street. I don't know your house number.'

'Annette, you don't need no number. You know Aboriginal house when you see it. Torn blinds at the window, lots of kids all over the yard, abandoned car on the front lawn, skinned kangaroo hang from the tree…' she said, with an infectious loud laugh.

The women had seriously big issues and big generous, humorous hearts.

Years later, I returned to Port Augusta and I was attracted by smoke coming from the backyard next door. I put my head over the fence and was amused to see a campfire nicely settling and my neighbours, a friendly indigenous family whose men had been out roo shooting during the night and had three kangaroos hanging by their tail on the rotary clothes line. Just like Lorna had described, he was skinning and butchering them. 'Come on over, missus, we're havin' barbecue, bring your own grog tho,' he said. It was a great Saturday afternoon.

Land rights for Aboriginal people were all abuzz around this time and Jesse, an Aboriginal woman, had five children staying at the shelter. She was thrilled her 'mob' were taking action. We applied to the Housing Trust Emergency Priority selection committee. We considered Jessie would get a house quicker than via application to the Aboriginal section.

She was refused. This rejection dumbfounded us. I had previously been reassured by the assistant manager, who I meet for coffee earlier, that our shelter women would be treated favourably from the Emergency Priority Committee.

I immediately rang the section and inquired why she was rejected.

They replied, 'When Jesse was asked did she have any other means to obtain a house, she told the interviewer her Uncle Scrubby was applying for land rights and he would get three million dollars and he would buy her a house!'

Jesse was very proud of her Uncle Scrubby.

It appeared to me that non-Aboriginal interviewers of the Emergency Priority were stupid, and a good reason to give Aboriginal women a special Aboriginal funded housing section. We sent her off to the Aboriginal Committee. Jesse finally got her special Aboriginal funded house.

*

There were no pensions for single mothers in those early days, and when single mother's pensions were introduced, they barely met their needs. I found many women who some years earlier had been able to escape wife-bashing had taken to prostitution to support their children, only to find they were prime targets to be bashed by customers and employers alike. Most worked in massage parlours and had regular hours, which helped with time management for their kids. Many arrived at the women's shelter after terrible bashings. They did not seek medical or police help. The shelter gave them respite. It was a time when prostitution was illegal – illegal for women, that is, not for their male customers. It was a time when men made the laws, men enforced the law, men prosecuted, men judged and men sought the services of the women, many of whom made a good living from these same men.

Customers included judges, lawyers, prosecutors, police, professional men – but it was only the women who were rounded up, prosecuted, fined, tainted and stigmatised as persons who acted illegally. It came a time when women began agitating for prostitution to be decriminalised and political debates raged on.

Several parliamentary inquiries were held and I made lengthy written submissions, as well as personal appearances before select committee proceedings supporting rights for women. The fight continues.

*

Gifts of money and other usable items were the mainstay for our survival during those early unfunded days, and continued to be for the life of the shelter. For several years, a fashionable women's clothing store located in Rundle Mall donated all the new clothes that were returned to the store. A missing button, a frayed hem needing a stitch or two were no problem and the women were grateful to have new clothes – something some women had not had for many years.

Wintertime was of concern – ensuring that all the resettled women and children had sufficient warm clothing, bedding and blankets. Each year *The Sunday Mail* ran a 'blanket appeal' and we received large boxes of old and new blankets to distribute to all the women we had in the community. We also used them at the shelter. That charity appeal was a lifesaver for us and we were grateful for their support.

Christmas was busy. Our childcare worker (funded separately from the federal government Office of Childhood Services) always put on a grand Christmas party for the children. One year, a young off-duty police officer arrived dressed as Father Christmas and handed out presents. The children were delighted. For several weeks beforehand, we staff were busy sorting donations and delivering Christmas presents to all the resettled women and children we had scattered around in the community. This young police officer's actions turned the tide for our police relations.

*

It was just after that Christmas that a meeting was called.

There had been many complaints about police from a number of women's shelters during the past years to the Department of Community Welfare. A significant conference was called for all shelters in South Australia to air their complaints. About twenty feisty radical feminist women, and some less so, from various shelters sat in a semicircle with dignitaries from the police department.

I had long given up on calling for police assistance. My early experiences had left me with little confidence that they would be of any help. As each shelter told their grievances, police of their district were given the opportunity to reply. There were many heated exchanges from the fierce feminists and the meeting was getting hot-headed and out of hand.

It came my time to tell about our experiences with police and I took a different tack. I could be seen as traitor to the aggrieved women, but with my tongue in my cheek, I told the story about our young police Father Christmas. Everyone in the room was gobsmacked.

Our local sergeant rose to reply. With gracious good humour, the poor guy mockingly apologised to his senior officers – it would do his reputation no good for it to be known among them that he and his team were friendly with the women from Naomi.

*

Sadly, at Christmas we were also inundated with new arrivals. Women with blackened eyes and crying children would arrive for a few days. Because their abuse happened due to alcohol-infused violence, many would excuse their partner's behaviour, saying it was the alcohol that was the problem. Some went home after a few days with hope: 'He won't be drinking now. It only happens when he's been drinking.' Some we saw back with us further down the track. Alcohol abuse does not cause domestic violence but the abuse is often acted out under the influence of it. Attacks also happen when the same perpetrator has not been drinking.

One Christmas, we had several dozens of frozen turkeys donated to us and little freezer space. With their use-by date approaching, we had difficulty in giving them all away. Many resettled women did not have refrigerators, and some had never had turkey and were unsure how to cook such a 'big chook'. We had turkey everywhere. We cooked as many as we could and handed them around.

We begged women to take the rest. 'Here! Have a turkey,' we said, as we thrust a frozen bird onto amazed women strangers. And weekend arrivals who left the shelter on Monday morning returned home with a defrosting turkey under their arm.

*

Easter was a pleasant time and many businesses donated boxes of Easter eggs for all the children. We staff played Easter bunny and managed to deliver all the chocolate eggs. We shared our oversupply of eggs with other shelters who were not so fortunate, and other shelters had their own way of dealing.

Women from one shelter, who shall remain anonymous, went begging to a supermarket for donations of Easter eggs and walked into a big display of chocolate eggs, slyly poking their fingers into soft chocolate, breaking a required number. A shelter worker asked the manager if they could have all the 'damaged' ones at a good discount price. He was glad to move the damaged eggs!

'Oops,' she said cheekily as she packed twenty or more damaged eggs into a bag…

It takes all kinds to survive.

*

There were days of shared sadness too. Mother's Day was always a difficult day. Our society advertises Mother's Day as a day of celebrating the joy of having children. At the shelter, many women spent the day crying about the children they had been forced to relinquish as unwed mothers, or the children left behind in the care of abusive husbands, or those in welfare care. Our mutual tears made me determined to keep my own family together. For a week each year, we suffered the 'celebrating' of Mother's Day.

*

I could not write a book about domestic violence without a space for child abuse. A whole book could be written about domestic violence and the serious high risks of child sexual abuse in a home.

Child abuse is an integral part of domestic violence. Child sexual abuse – 'incest' from 'high-end' abusers, paedophile fathers/father figures – is inevitable and operates within the secret of domestic violence. All child abuse is equally a part of domestic violence and neither should be considered any worse than the other – for all children living in a home with domestic violence suffer abuse, which doesn't necessarily have to be physical, though much of it is. And sexual abuse is not limited to physical contact. Children can be abused in many different ways and corrupted by giving them or subtly exposing them to pornography.

Sexual abuse is a controlled and premeditated crime, supported by grooming, planning and many lies. Paedophile fathers and stepfathers and grandfathers feel safe (age is no barrier to paedophile perpetrators), grooming, acting behind closed doors, protected by the image of fatherhood and parenting and family care. They all know a child will not tell. And mothers are mostly subdued and unaware. It is a secret within a secret. Child sexual abuse is not just about sex, it is 'character homicide', for it destroys a child's ability to mature and trust as they should; it changes who they are meant to be and there are other lifelong issues for victims. Many child victims succumb to the pain as an adult and commit suicide. Other do not reach adulthood – teenage suicides happen and the community wonders why.

With this in mind, I wonder whether some teenage suicides that are contributed to school yard bullying are in fact dues to domestic violence in the first degree. (This might be too much for parents to consider.) I was aware that more than one teenage child committed suicide as a result of sexual abuse. And more than one left the shelter undisclosed to us.

In 1978, Cindy came and stayed a few days and then went to another shelter. I am ashamed to say I was uncertain of her story of being sexually abused by her doctor father. She was just fifteen years old and came from a wealthy family in the eastern suburbs; she went to an expensive prestigious school. The father was interviewed and believed. Cindy was forced to return home.

'You were not the only one to have doubts about her. The other shelter also had doubts. She took her own life,' a visiting health worker told me.

Her words that I was not alone in my doubt gave me no relief. I decided there and then never to ever doubt a child's story.

For many young girls, sexual abuse by their biological father can continue beyond childhood and into young adulthood. It is more common than generally known.

Irene, forty-five years of age, was a mother of three children who had been experiencing domestic violence all her married life. It came as a shock to her to find that her eighteen-year-old daughter Tracy was stealing her clothes. First it was borrowing her T-shirts, then her socks, and as time went by she just helped herself to whatever she wanted. Irene challenged Tracy about taking her underpants and a big fight blew up. Irene's husband joined in with a torrent of abuse towards her, and a full-scale domestic violent episode erupted. Irene fled to Naomi Women's Shelter in tears. She had, for many years, been treated with contempt by her husband and children. Mothers lose their position of authority in domestic violence.

After a few days, Irene returned home. Two weeks later, she was back.

When Irene returned home, she found her daughter had moved into the double bed she shared with her husband. Irene was relegated to her daughter's bed. The husband and daughter were now living as man and wife. All Irene's possessions – her clothes, jewellery, family photos, everything – were taken from her by her daughter over a period of time. Irene was forced out of her home by both her daughter and her husband. The eighteen-year-old Tracy took over the role and life of her mother.

Irene stayed with us for a long while then moved on.

Lynnette was forty-nine years old when she left her husband. She became aware her husband had been sexually abusing her daughter, Carol when she was twelve or thirteen years old. When Carol grew up and had two small children, shel provoked huge animosity towards her mother and broke all ties with her. Lynnette could not understand why her adult daughter preferred to engage with her father, who had sexually abused her. The adult Carol was blackmailing her father for money. The father paid the money and they continued the relationship for years.

Lynnette lives alone, with no family, and has no communication with her grandchildren from her other children.

Media tend to lump all childhood sexual abuse together, whether it be from stranger paedophiles or from institution staff. But it is my belief that children abused in a family home are different. They have nowhere to run, no one to tell; they are captured into the culture of secrets. If adults have difficulty telling a stranger, it is no easier for a child to do so.

Not all children who are abused grow up and continue relationships with their abuser, but many do. It is the abuser who continues to keep his trained victim, his disciple, emotionally bonded into his cult of abuse. 'Catch them young and train them' is the chauvinist cult maxim.

All child abuse destroys lives. Some children grow to overcome their childhood trauma, but not without many years of help, self-help and self-determination, and they never totally forget. They, like their abused mothers, have debilitating flashbacks forever.

It has become a controversy that some adult children who report child sexual abuse from their fathers when they have grown up and disclose incidents of sexual abuse as a child, are not always believed.

The questions turn to 'Why did you take so long to tell?' The term 'false memory' is slipping into use and is a concern for the victims. Some children suffer unbelievable degradations which only come to emotional realisation when the adult child experiences some other current adult life crisis. In my view, it is unsafe to ignore them and their disclosed history.

Almost all the women who came to the women's shelter had a story of child sexual abuse. It was so prevalent we lost count and gave up trying to have child abuse/sexual abuse dealt with by the authorities, as no one would listen. 'You have no proof', 'Where is the evidence' we were told. The best we could do was support the mothers, who, in turn, supported the child.

Over the years, hundreds of stories have come my way, and it is good to know victims are at last being heard. But in my opinion there still is not enough attention given to children living with domestic violence and the 'secret within a secret' children are forced to carry throughout their lives. Shame holds them prisoned.

Some adult victims never tell even their own husbands, and carry on feeling shame all their lives. They are at great pains to keep and hide the secret. They carry the same shame we of earlier generations suffered. Rape victims and sexual abuse in domestic violence carries unspeakable shame and loss of self-esteem for victims, and most victims are held 'emotional secret' prisoners for life. We hear much about the brutal assaults, but we do not hear about the biggest secret of them all: 'Because he is my father.'

*

Mothers of children who are sexually abused are often blamed for knowing and doing nothing to protect a child. I have a different view.

Most mothers are unaware their children are being abused. It is one of the 'secret' parts of the assailant's repertoire, his clever cunning, to act in secret. But when mothers did find out, many gave this as the reason for coming to the shelter. 'He can abuse me all he likes, but when he starts on the kids...' Mothers, who themselves have been abused as children, are more aware and on the lookout, but for mothers who have no such experience, it is almost impossible to grasp. Who will believe them?

Family courts have accused women of being vindictive, others say they have no proof and children are prisoners to the lies and the secrets.

The ages of the children we saw varied. One was a baby of three months. There seemed to be some fathers who were quick to start sexually with very young primary school-age children, while others preferred older early teenage children. All children were groomed early almost from the time they met their biological father, stepfather or grandfather.

'I don't know how old I was when it started, I only know how old I was when it stopped – when I left home at sixteen,' a twenty-five-year-old woman told me.

I do not advocate taking children away from mothers. Take the father away and charge him with domestic violence!

*

Mothers who are unable to care and protect themselves are not likely to be able to protect their children. There is nowhere to hide in a violent home.

In recent years, I saw a woman I recognised on the television news, who was leaving court with her adult daughters after their father had been convicted of sexually abusing her three girls. I went to see her and she was devastated and could hardly speak. She had no idea what had been happening to the children. In her marriage, she had become irrelevant and treated with disdain by both her husband and the three little girls under five years old. She was nothing more than their abused housemaid. She cried as she struggled to tell me.

On many occasions, she would be in the kitchen washing the dishes, her husband sitting on a chair, and he would have the little girls sitting in a row on the dining table teaching them to read. 'Good girl. Good girl,' she heard him say. But she did not know he had his fingers in their vaginas as he praised them.

The little girls adored him and they were constantly by his side. The mother was forced out of the home and remarried. As the girls grew, they refused to have anything to do with her. She had thought they were a happy family. The girls contacted her when they reported their childhood abuse to the police and their mother supported them during the court hearings, but a short time later they returned to their feelings of contempt for her.

Their mother was invited to apply for Victims of Crime compensation, but her daughters angrily protested.

'I don't know what to do. My girls are so angry at me. They say I'm not entitled to anything.'

I told her she should apply for it. 'It's recognition for all the other suffering mothers who have no such opportunity.'

I felt it was similar to honouring women in history who fought for our right to vote. I pleaded with her to apply and she eventually did. Her relationship with one daughter is wobbly and, with the other two, non-existent.

The girls could never understand why their mother 'allowed' what the father did to them, and did not understand how the mother could know nothing. They didn't understand that their mother was his victim before them and she was powerless. It is the same story for most mothers whose children are abused/sexually abused by their fathers.

Powerless people, victim-mothers are often held in contempt by others; they are seen as weak, at fault, and pathetic. While violent abusers are seen as strong, winners, and safe to be with, they are cheered on as in sporting heroes. Charming charismatic and good-looking abusers attract similar success.

*

I was amazed when one mother, Patsy, told me that when she found out her husband was sexually abusing her children, she kicked him out instantly. I had never heard of this instant eviction happening before. I had great admiration for her.

It all happened by accident. The near teenage son Tony, and teenage daughter Sheena were arguing, but something didn't sound right, so Patsy stepped in and demanded to know what the fight was about. Sheena refused to say anything, and the mother sent the younger boy off to his room.

Patsy persisted with her questioning until the girl finally screamed at her, 'You know. You know.'

Patsy was shocked and baffled. 'What do I know that I don't know?' Patsy thought, and asked more questions trying to establish the answer. Had Tony done something?

'You know,' was all Sheena would say.

Patsy was shocked and asked more questions, but the girl only screamed, 'You know, you know.'

Patsy would not leave the couch and made her daughter sit, until finally Sheena told: her father was sexually abusing her. The father was standing in the doorway and heard the girl's confession. The mother looked up and saw him standing there, and she didn't hesitate. She told him to 'Get out – get out now!' Patsy threatened police action and he couldn't leave quick enough.

I was very impressed with her bravery and swift action. Patsy and her husband had a large mortgage and other financial problems, but she ignored these concerns and acted immediately to protect her daughter. Sadly, she was too late: the damage to her daughter was done.

Patsy said she was shocked later when she realised what she had done. 'I was terrified about how I'd cope.'

Her husband was later taken to court and convicted, after the adult children gave evidence. Another child in the family who had left home was also abused but she did not tell. Now the father lives with another woman and her children!

Patsy was also invited to apply for Victim of Crimes compensation and she had the same response from the children – demanding she not apply. I put on my big feminist hat and pleaded with her to validate her motherhood. She eventually applied and I was surprised by her strong reaction to receiving a small cash compensation.

I thought it was a big win for mothers, but she had a different view. She was glad her children received compensation money, which validated them as being victims, but she said she was pissed off for receiving compensation for what he did to the kids. They could take him to court, but she wasn't able to do so for what he did to her.

I reckon she has a point.

Patsy describes her current relationship with the children as 'like walking on eggshells'.

*

Many children do try to tell their mothers, but they use language that is vague and inconclusive. It would be helpful if we could find a way to teach children universal language, language that would make it clear what is happening to them.

'You don't know what's going on in your own home' can be difficult to interpret as 'I'm being sexually abused.'

A small trickle of adult children are coming forward, but for them it is too late. Childhood has been missed. They have suffered long and now carry severe personality disorders, depression, alcohol and drug abuse, other self-harming behaviours and several failed relationships. Some waver for years before they settle to a 'normal' life. And mothers are cast asunder; they are left to grieve the loss of a family that is no more.

*

The sisters Jenny and Ann, who were waiting for their father to be prosecuted for sexual abuse and who were under my care as their guardian, were still living with us at Naomi Women's Shelter and had no financial support at all.

One morning an older woman, who had been bashed by her adult son, arrived from interstate. She had spent the night and stopped me in the passage the next morning and asked how much she had to pay for her stay. I told her that accommodation was free.

'No,' she said. 'I have to pay you.'

I tried to explain, then I backed off quickly as she interrupted me.

'How dare you! How dare you make me accept charity? I'm sixty years old and I've never accepted charity in all my life. You have no right to put me in that position now! I will pay for my accommodation.'

I was perplexed, but I did understand. My parents would have said something like that.

Just then, as the woman was dipping her hand into her purse, Jenny and Ann came walking down the passage. I grabbed their arms.

'Look. These young girls are living here. They can't go home and have no money to buy any personal items. If it makes you feel better, you could give them some money.'

She slowly looked them up and down contemplating their situation, then smiled and said, 'I'd be delighted to, my dear. Thank you so much.'

The girls put up their hands to decline. They did not want to accept money from an 'old lady' but I interrupted with 'Please, help me out here, girls, and take it,' and they did.

The problem solved, I felt chuffed. The woman paid her way, the girls got some pocket money and I did not have to write receipts or run to the bank for a few dollars. Old habits die hard!

*

Late in 1976, I did something I was very pleased to be part of. I helped the women from my home town of Port Augusta to establish a women's shelter. I invited Deborah McCulloch, women's advisor to the premier, to come as a guest speaker to a women's dinner at a local hotel. My sister Dianne, then married and living in Port Augusta, called a public meeting to formalise a group as a steering committee. They applied for federal funding and were granted it under the new system for funding shelters.

These Port Augusta women were far from feminists and they were too late to help the older Mrs McKenzies of the town, but I was very glad that my home town, where I had first experienced wife-bashing, now had a women's shelter.

Soon after the Port Augusta shelter got started, Dianne separated from her husband and moved to Adelaide and stayed with me.

It was not long before Mack came running up to me and said, 'Your sister is coming on to me and if you don't want any trouble, you should get rid of her.'

Family members are not wanted. They cannot be trusted to secrecy. They have not come under the cult spell of influence.

*

Naomi Women's Shelter brought a variety of new social issues to light as women began to come for help in a number of areas other than violent domestic abuse. But the stories of suicide, incest, rape, abortion, confinement and torture kept coming. The stories did not all come from women victims, either.

None was more surprising than a man who told me how his marriage came about and his wife's subsequent behaviour. His wife was young and pregnant when they married. He had been reluctant to get married, but both his mother-in-law and his fiancée had insisted. Soon after the marriage, she had their first son and then a year later gave birth to their second. Her behaviour as his wife distressed him. As he talked, I saw some similarities to the behaviour of some of the shelter women and I asked him if maybe she was behaving that way because she had been sexually abused by her father. He was silent and did not offer an opinion.

He returned some time later to tell me that he had confronted his mother-in-law and she had confessed that her husband had known her daughter sexually and that the firstborn boy was actually the father's. A hasty marriage had had to be arranged. The man had been blindly talked into raising the son of his father-in-law. This innocent man's marriage was a desperately unhappy one. He had been caught up in the lies and deceits around another family's domestic violence and child sexual abuse.

Other women also told me stories of secretly having their father's child. Some raised them, others had their babies adopted.

*

Another story came from a grandmother who was caring for her son's two daughters after the son had finally left his violent wife. The grandmother's side of the family had no history or experience of domestic violence and had been shattered by the marriage of their son into violence. His dysfunctional wife was the daughter of a violent man and had grown up with violence. She bashed her children and abused her husband. She constantly attacked her husband's mother (the grandmother of the story) and verbal abuse, foul language, harassment and even physical attacks were directed at the son's parents. The grandmother, telling me the story, was deeply saddened by how one abused person could have such a dramatic impact on the lives of so many of her unsuspecting, innocent new family.

*

Not all mothers live with their abusers. Many separated women living in a new home often feel the need for their child to have contact with their father. Family courts also oblige mothers to permit fathers to have access to children. This order often gives abusive fathers opportunities to continue the abuse.

'Why do you allow him in your home?' I asked one woman. The man had been entering her home and abusing for several years.

'Because he's their father,' she said.

I had heard from many mothers who were constantly intimidated by resentful abusive husbands. Abusers continue their abuse with well-developed cunning and subtle actions. They intimidate and use children to pass on messages. They coerce children with extravagant presents and exciting outings that intimidate and undermine a mother.

One man I knew walked into his former partner's home and helped himself to whatever he wanted – mostly to intimidate. He emptied the fridge, took books, used her computer, took her car – anything that would upset her. Any new court orders were ignored. Such men are difficult to defuse, and women are too afraid to resist or complain. Mostly the women have had insufficient time to recover or 'de-program' from years of previous abuse and are powerless to prevent it. Courts and police rarely understand that although women may be separated for several years, they are still vulnerable to abuse from persistent abusers.

Similarly, women who are insufficiently recovered are vulnerable to other predators who move in on them. Some women see a new relationship as a way of curtailing their current assailant. After a while, if the new relationship proves to be abusive, the women is trapped again.

Proper and appropriate recovery, maybe taking several years, is absolutely necessary for victims to gain control over their own lives and gather strength to protect their children. As a rule of thumb, it could be one year of recovering, with appropriate help, for every three years of abuse. Victims of long-term abuse never fully recover; there is always residue. Some past victims may not think so, but look deeper and you will see. Eating disorders, problem gambling, mental illness, excessive retail therapy, prescription drug abuse, and so on.

Children who live their entire childhood in abuse also need many years of professional help to recover from the trauma of family dysfunction. Children are the forgotten group when it comes to the future needs of victims of domestic violence and abuse. They suffer depression, behavioural problems, eating disorders, drug abuse – the list is long and society silently looks on.

The problem often spreads through the neighbourhood when distressed children next door create surrounding mayhem.

*

I answered the telephone to a screaming woman's voice

'I've been kidnapped. I've escaped. I'm frightened. He'll come after me. I can't stay here long.' She was hysterical.

I asked her where she was and called a taxi to collect her from the street corner she nominated. We were waiting for her out the front of the shelter. Once again, the taxi driver asked for no payment when she said she had no money. Scantily dressed, she stumbled out and was quickly wrapped in a blanket by caring hands and shuffled inside to fireside coffee and biscuits. She was shaking, crying, eyes darting all over the place. She would burst out with some words then her eyes glazed over and stared. I did my best to reassure her she was now safe.

Finally, she recovered enough to speak. She had come to Adelaide to marry a man she had got to know in Melbourne. When she arrived at his flat, he had tied her wrists and ankles to the four bedposts. Then he had brought in men to have sex with her, lots of men, day and night. She had cigarette burns on the soles of her feet and shallow puncture marks on her legs. Her wrists and ankles were red and rubbed raw.

For several days, she didn't leave her room. She remained huddled on her bed. She couldn't talk to anyone and did not come out for food. She was dazed and seemed to be in a trance. She slept on and off for days. We saw to her needs and kept up a food and drink service, which one unkind social worker chastised us for, saying we were pandering to her and she was using us. Back then, no one wanted to believe such stories, even some other resident women. But I never doubted she had been kept, tortured and raped as she told us.

When she did eventually venture out, she always wanted someone with her. She took two weeks to recover sufficiently to consider what she might do next. We were able to contact her parents and helped her to be reunited with her family.

*

During the life of the women's shelter, it was a time when society took the view that wives in marriage could not be raped and, indeed, many raped women succumbed to the notion that 'It's what you're supposed to do.' But we were hearing bizarre stories of terrible degrading assaults. We began having round-the-kitchen-table conversations about being raped at home by husbands. We began by defining what that meant – leaving out the 'what you are supposed to do' bit – and were shocked to find all the women had been raped – that is, forced to have sex with their husbands when they were not consenting. Many women told of unwanted horrific and vile sadistic acts on married women. Many sex acts were from copycat images from the man's collection of pornography. Husbands considered wives were for their own pleasure, to do whatever they wanted.

At this time, the state government was struggling to introduce appropriate legislation to protect married women.

In those days, rape by a person known to the woman was often turned round to blame the woman, and her whole sexual experience was put on trial. Therefore, many women never reported the assault.

The Naomi Women's Shelter put in a call for a 'rape within marriage' clause, after several stories such as those that follow.

Maureen was thirty-five and the mother of three children. 'Rape! Oh, yer – he threw me against the wall, pulled off me clothes, ripped them, and I thought he was going to rape me again. Instead, he threw me onto the floor, emptied a plate of spaghetti over me and held me down so his big Alsatian could lick me and have sex with me. When he went to work, I grabbed the kids and went to a service station and hitched a ride with a truckie all the way to Adelaide. Of course, that bugger wanted his reward too, and now I need a doctor.'

Karen was forty-five and the mother of teenage children. 'No, I've never been raped by him. But he wants sex every night and I can't stand it. I say no, but he takes no notice, and if I don't let him, he belts me.'

Not all women claimed they were raped with violence, but many complained they were expected to be available any time he wanted, and after many years of constant demands felt they had been abused over and over again, year after year, children and more children. Passive rape is still rape. And it still happens today, perhaps minus the many children, but women still suffer sexual abuse in relationships.

Many teenage girls were raped by their boyfriends and came to the shelter. They were afraid of their attacker and many never reported the rape. And for those who did report, the ordeal of police investigations and prosecution procedures was harrowing for victims. Their traumas were not understood. We received many phone calls from distressed girls and were acting as a rape crisis centre.

Women from the women's movement were talking about setting up such a centre. They were slow to act and we at Naomi decided to give them a hurry-up by announcing we too would apply for funds to establish a rape crisis centre. That got them moving and they managed to organise and establish a centre at Hindmarsh. The state government had moves under way to have a 'rape in marriage' clause included in the Criminal Crimes Act and women from the shelter gave testimony of their experiences. They helped move the push for legislation.

Many other new initiatives for women were being established during the time Don Dunstan was Premier of South Australia. Deborah McCulloch, the premier's advisor, supported the women's shelters. She did, however, have a difficult time keeping the women's groups united as they became ever more fractious. I moved away from the general meeting of the women's movement at Bloor Court. There, issues were growing on career structures in the public service and the education system. In my view, they were more middle-class issues.

I was entrenched in my support of the women I worked with in the shelter. It was obvious they knew what they needed, and I was determined to listen to them. I also kept up my activities within the Labor Party, making waves for women to be elected as candidates. My impatient, militant voice was a thorn in their side and I was losing ground, quickly becoming out of favour.

*

With our new commercial-size laundry at the Naomi Women's Shelter in Prospect, as mentioned earlier, we had invited women who could not afford washing machines to bring their washing with them when they came to visit.

Bonny, a weekly visitor, was an older woman who had been to the shelter for many respite visits. She had an eleven-year-old son called Gerald, who came with her. He was already showing signs of anger and violence and was a big disruption at the shelter. Some interstate shelters did not accept boys over ten years old for that reason, as they could sometimes begin to be violent.

She was a regular, back and forth, to and from the shelter. She just could not make the break from her abusive husband. She was getting desperate and becoming quite irrational. Each time she left the shelter, she would still return often for a chat.

On one daytime visit, she told me it was 'Tuesday curry night'—she cooked curry every Tuesday because curry disguised the rat poison she was feeding her husband. My ears pricked up. We were used to hearing all kinds of ways desperate women fantasised to get rid of their abusers. Most were outrageous, funny and spoken in jest, so we just laughed at Bonny. Until the next week, when Bonny had a super-size box of rat poison in her basket, and again the following week when Bonny said he was sick and went to the doctor.

When Bonny left, I felt awful and afraid for him and her. What could I do? First, I rang the poison unit at the hospital and asked them about rat poison. 'No, it won't kill him, but it will make him sick.' I felt relieved.

Next week, Bonny came with another box of rat poison and I told her, 'Stop wasting your money, Bonny. You'll only make him sick and get yourself in big trouble.' I managed to convince her and she left the rat poison in the office.

Two or three weeks later, Bonny arrived to stay, but without her son this time. She had a black eye and a suitcase.

'Oh! Bonny what happened? And where's Gerald?'

'I left him home. He's as bad as his father, abusing me. And that bastard, he's been in a mad rage – he reckons I'm trying to poison him. Ha! He says the curry doesn't taste as good as it used to. He liked the curry with the rat poison.'

We were all relieved. Poor Bonny! But at least she wasn't feeding him poison any more. Injured as she was, she could see the funny side, and we all had a laugh with her – I still shudder when the local hotel advertises their special 'Tuesday curry nights'!

*

I later realised that Bonny's behaviour was consistent with women expressing the 'revenge' emotion that so often accompanies women who feel powerless in domestic violence. These emotions are often misunderstood by helping agencies. Victims of other crimes are often recorded as saying words of malice about what they would do to an offender. And where the offender is dealt with under the law and there is a satisfactory court outcome, victims and relatives often express feelings of relief and closure. There is no such opportunity in law available to victims of domestic violence. Women are often pilloried if they dare to utter words of revenge when they are expressing their frustrations at the injustice they feel.

Others are told they are vindictive for reporting child abuse.

'You are just a vindictive woman,' I heard one judge say to a woman who was trying to tell of her child being sexually abused.

*

The Naomi Women's Shelter was a curiosity for social workers. Several came calling. Some were pests but some were genuinely intrigued. I was not fond of social workers back then. I saw them as mostly middle-class women and sexist men, imposing their own attitudes as solutions to problems they did not understand. They often did not believe the women's stories and treated them like wayward children. They seemed to me to serve little purpose.

One eager social worker came to the shelter to see a woman. 'If there is anything I can do for you,' she offered.

'No,' replied the woman. 'I'm getting all the help I need from the shelter. But wait, there is something I want.'

The social worker was delighted. 'Yes?' she said with enthusiasm.

'I need a house,' said the woman.

'Oh, I'm sorry. As the staff can tell you, we can't supply houses. But if there's anything else…'

'Why yes…'

The social worker regained her eagerness.

'I need more money.'

'Oh! I'm sorry, as the staff can tell you, we can't supply you with more money.'

'Well then, you can't help me, 'cos that's all I need. Just a house and more money. The other things are being supplied to me here at the shelter.'

The women became a little bit weary of all the attention. 'Being looked at like animals in a zoo,' they called it.

A senior social worker rang and asked if she could come and 'have a look'. The women had their own suggestion, which I passed on to the social worker: 'You can come and look at us if we can come to your place and look at you.' That did not go down well, and I was later to learn that social worker was assigned to 'keep an eye on us' and reported to our funding agent. I had made another enemy.

*

I was aware of possible medical problems arising and was always on guard for children's dysentery. From the first day of operation at Naomi, we had a 'barrier nursing' practice of putting all the used dishes in a bucket of disinfectant to be soaked for several hours before they were washed up and air-dried (no dirty tea towels) and then put away. We had no problems with illness or sick children until…

A doctor came to the shelter one day. He said he would be happy to call and attend to the women and children. He did not have a practice and he had time. I gave him permission to call. From then on, he was always at the shelter, handing out prescriptions for everything. With a doctor in charge of the shelter's health, our infection control methods slackened and dysentery slipped in.

I was unaware that the doctor was calling almost every day and was asking about new arrivals. His visits were increasing and he always produced his Medicare claim forms and passed them around for women to sign. Women began to complain.

'What game are you playing?' One street-wise woman confronted me and I realised that she thought the doctor must be paying me to let him in.

I was shocked and took immediate action to stop him. I told him that we would call him if he was needed. I wrote a letter of complaint to the Medical Board about the extent to which he was handing around his Medicare forms. I was particularly peeved because we were struggling with a multitude of distressed children and we were begging government for funds to provide children with special staff and this man was attracting money with ease, seemingly for no reason. Medicare never spoke to any of the women and the Medical Board said there was no case to prove that he was acting improperly.

I was to pay dearly later for my interference in his easy business. My lesson with him was, never come between a man and his money. I later learnt that he had managed to get a job with a public service. I was appalled.

While the doctor was coming regularly, we had many cases of child dysentery. After I stopped him, we went back to the old home-nursing trick – a dishes in bucket with disinfectant regime – and we cleaned up the problem.

*

In middle 1976 and into 1977, the two sisters Jenny and Ann were still with us. They were being stalked by their dangerous, angry father and brother and we had to be particularly vigilant for their safety. We were waiting the announcement of a prosecution, but it was taking a long time. The girls' plight created awareness that other girls who were running from sexual abuse had nowhere to go. Many were simply living on the streets and were creating a social problem. With the onset of winter, the shelter saw an influx of kids.

With our publicly donated money, I rented a cottage in Brompton not far from Naomi and set up a place for them. I visited the kids' house every morning and one morning it was packed with street kids. There were about twenty of them camped all over the house. Boys and girls were running away from abuse. Many were using drugs and I had no idea how to cope with them. The house was too small and we had to change.

One of the women from Naomi agreed to live in and be a house mother. And a few months later, our young schoolteacher woman worker at the shelter (funded from a grant from the federal Office of Child Care) shared her wages with a male youth worker and with publicly donated money we set up a bigger house in Torrensville, a shelter for teenage homeless kids. They called it Kelly's Kid Shelter, after my blue heeler dog Kelly, who had had eleven puppies. The shelter lasted until the workers were exhausted and Naomi could no longer keep up the financial support.

After a while, another woman schoolteacher I knew set up a home for young girls in her own rented home and Jenny and Ann went to live with her. They were there for two or three years. Having a place to send girls lifted the burden from Naomi but we were still inundated with women and their children. The children were by far the greatest number of residents and many mothers were afraid to let them go to the local school. My solution was to employ a schoolteacher and run our own lessons. We had a succession of three very hard-working teachers who were loved by the children and when we got a small bus took the children on day trips.

It was around this time that I noticed Mack being cruel to our family dog Kelly. I couldn't watch this cruelty and arranged another home for her. The children were upset and I made the excuse that Kelly did not like the boy next door and she might try to bite him. We later had another dog called Douglas but he was also being harmed. I had to find a new home for him too.

*

Even though the two girls were in a safe home, I kept in touch with the police, regarding the prosecution of their father. On 10 August 1976, I wrote to the Attorney General, Peter Duncan, and requested an explanation why Mr Brian had not been charged. I received a reply on 21 September from the Chief Secretary saying that the Welfare Department had visited Mr Brian and there had been insufficient evidence to obtain a conviction.

What? How could this be happening? If two girls from the same family gave individual statements that corroborated each other, why could that not be sufficient evidence? What hope would one child have? The girls were devastated. They were worried about their little sister, still at home and nothing was being done. Five years later, the mother was charged and imprisoned for killing the father. She was sentenced to life.

I was appalled at the injustice of her sentence and called on the women's movement to muster a campaign to free the mother Mrs Davies from prison. I begged the editors of the *Advertiser* daily newspaper to support our campaign and they obliged. The mother was eventually freed. The girls Jenny and Ann told their stories to the press to help their mother. She was eventually freed but the sisters were consequently ostracised from their family forever. The ordeal took its toll. In following years, the girls took their lives, one after the other. It is the saddest case I have ever known. It is a horrific testimony to the longevity and suffering created by domestic violence and child abuse.

Around 1977–8, Jenny and Ann pleaded with us at the shelter to abduct their little sister, who would have been about twelve years old then. We set out a plan and made several attempts. The child was always under guard. A prisoner of her family. Our rescue attempts failed.

*

The Naomi Shelter itself did not always escape the front page of the newspapers. 'Fake Nurse Abducts Boy' was the frontline news story in August 1980. The newspaper carried the story for several days.

Unbeknown to us in the Naomi office, a, newly arrived mother of a boy, had taken her two-year-old to the Children's Hospital. He was constipated. She returned without her child. I found the mother crying, extremely distressed. She told me that she had left her home state several weeks previously with paperwork from a judge of the Family Court, giving her interim custody of her son while the custody case was going on. She moved from one state and shelter to another avoiding her perpetrator. He had been staking out the shelter for two days even before she arrived. He got lucky and when she left the shelter he followed her to the hospital.

The child was given an enema and all was well until mother and child walked out of the hospital. The perpetrator jumped out at her and snatched the boy from her arms. The mother screamed and there was a loud fracas outside and on the steps of the hospital. The fracas escalated and the hospital staff and police got involved.

The mother did not have her interim custody papers with her. The perpetrator had been to the local magistrate's court a few days previously and was armed with his new interim custody papers. These had been acquired without the judge being aware of the interstate family court orders and were based on misleading and false information. Federal court matters override state matters. Nonetheless, the police decided the perpetrator should take the child and did not give the woman time to produce her papers.

The hospital doctor decided to admit the child as a 'social admittance' and the perpetrator was allowed to sit guard over the child while the mother was sent away. This is an example of agency abuse, where a woman fleeing from abuse is often subjected to further abuse from agencies making their own judgements, not listening to the woman's story and deciding against the woman. It was a frequent occurrence.

The shelter women were incensed that the mother was being denied rightful custody of her boy. We hatched our fightback plan. We would simply walk into the hospital, cause a distraction and collect the child from under the nose of the perpetrator. Four of us rode to the hospital and parked the car at the back entrance. Acting brilliantly, our 'nurse' told the perpetrator she needed to take the boy for a blood test. She picked him up, walked to the elevators and handed the boy to his mother in the elevator. She and I drove hastily back to the shelter. The heist took less than fifteen minutes from the shelter to the hospital and back to the shelter.

The mother phoned the hospital and later the police and said her son was safely with her but that did not stop the police and the hospital from creating media frenzy around the incident. Later that evening, hoping to dampen the media hype of claims of a hospital 'inside job' kidnapping a child, I rang the police and told them we had organised the heist. I was mightily put out when a senior officer refused to believe me, saying it could not have been us – it had been a professional inside hospital job. At the word 'professional' I felt chuffed. But, because he would not believe it was us, I had to tell him how we did it, when, what timing and so on and I also told him why we took the child. He was hard to convince. In fact, he was not even interested in the history of child sexual abuse. That was typical in those days. He was annoyed by us shelter women being so brazen – not to mention successful.

'My God, Annette,' he finally conceded, 'that's something from *Starsky and Hutch*.'

'Excuse me! If you don't mind, don't give this credit to blokes. If you must go to film actors, at least give us women a Laverne and Shirley credit.'

As far as I was concerned, it was simple. The woman had a valid legitimate court order from the Family Court in Canberra and we had her story. The mother was free to travel anywhere she chose. But what we did not know was that a very well-respected interstate journalist, who is still working today, had been following the story. She rang us to tell us just how devious this predator was. She told us he had enacted the same scenario with another woman at another hospital interstate and had taken her two boys to a secret isolated farm where they were being held against family court orders. There were animals, pornographic photos taken and sold on to like-minded, perverted persons. From this scene of horror, our woman had rescued her child and ended up in our shelter.

During the increasing hysteria of the media, the mother was forced by police to give over the boy to the predator. She and I immediately flew to her home state and saw the judge who was dealing with the case. The judge was scathing of the predator's wrongdoing. The mother was eventually issued with full custody and the boy was returned to her.

How much more convoluted could a case be, when it was really just so obviously simple to see what was going on? Until women are listened to and believed, this type of injustice, not to mention abuse of children, will continue.

*

In 1977, three years after I established South Australia's first official women's shelter, I authored the Naomi Report. During the second year of the Naomi Shelter I could stand it no longer, having to constantly answer questions such as do women really get bashed? Are there really that many women who do? Why do women come to the shelter? So, I produced the Naomi Report. None of us at the shelter had any report-writing skills, but together with the staff and residents, we set out to record and make known as much as we could about the shelter.

The main objective was to tell the women's stories. It was a simple, primary school effort in which we put compiled statistics and retold women's own stories in straight-forward language. The report was produced and limited copies were published by friends and distributed. It was and still is the only public document with such information relevant to that time.

*

With reports published and conferences being organised, we shelter organisers were bound to come under government scrutiny. By 1977–78, the number of women's shelters around Australia had doubled and an interstate network between shelters was established. We gave women the opportunity to flee interstate to a safe place when there was serious and immediate danger. We had interstate conferences regularly. Our funding was never a certainty and we needed women close to the sources of funding to understand our predicament. These feminist women employed by the federal government attended our conferences and kept us abreast of inner government plans.

At one such conference in Canberra, I was taking a breather in the lounge area when I was approached by two very friendly-looking male public servants.

'What's going on in there?' one asked casually.

'Who's asking?'

'We're from the Office of Information.'

Mmm, I thought, there is no Office of Information.

'ASIO?'

'Yes, that's right.'

'Well, you won't get much from this lot. They only decide matters by consensus. No one in there is agreeing on anything right now.'

But the government, now run by Malcolm Fraser, began to show an interest in what we women were up to and wanted inside information.

A few weeks later, back at the shelter, we had a phone call from a woman who purported to come from the Canberra Office of Information. She asked if she could come and interview us about women's housing needs. She spent a whole day with us and her questions were anything but housing questions. Instead, in a very clumsy way, she asked about our sexual preferences, our future political campaigns, our policies and what political party we supported. That waved a red flag to me and I finally ignored her and left her with the staff, who were less guarded than me. They invited her to our prearranged restaurant dinner that night.

Later that evening, Mack called at the restaurant and settled for coffee. Always suspicious, he managed to sit next to her and began grilling her, questioning and badgering about why she had come to Adelaide.

'There's no Information Office. You're from ASIO, aren't you?' he accused her belligerently.

'No, I'm not.'

He wouldn't accept that and kept at her until she broke down and cried, big sobbing tears. I was shocked put my arm around her and told him to leave her be.

'She's lying. She's here as a spy. Liars always cry when they're found out.' It was a phrase he often used.

*

At the beginning of the 1980,s unemployment and homelessness was rising to new heights. We at Naomi were seeing a new dimension of need for shelters not just for domestic violence but for homelessness in general and especially for whole families. Fathers were pulling up in their cars out the front of Naomi and asking for assistance; the family breadwinner was unemployed and the family had been evicted from their home – they had been living in their car for several months. Children were dirty, hungry and unschooled. We heard stories from families, similar to those of the 1930s Great Depression, where women and children were evicted and whole families lived in tents along the Torrens River and I wondered how this sort of thing could be happening now. More and more fathers were asking Naomi to take in their wives and children while they sought accommodation and food from the Salvation Army Men's Shelter.

The federal government had allocated funds for the state government to set up homeless persons' accommodation but nothing was happening for families, and anything that was, was organised by the churches and was for men. Homeless persons gathered in large numbers where soup kitchens were operating and the homeless were setting up tent cities on the grass in the city square. We at Naomi were being inundated with requests for help, not just from women, but for entire families as well as single homeless persons. We helped out with blankets and food, but that was not enough – families needed to stay together.

Somewhere in this homeless emergency we were notified that a government-owned mansion named Kumanka in North Adelaide was sitting vacant. We directed families to the vacant house. They pitched tents on the front lawns and we then assisted with requests for bedding, blankets and food. Somehow people gained access to the house and we supported them.

To draw attention and help from the state government of the plight of these destitute and homeless families we launched a campaign to invite members of parliament and the press to the opening of Kumanka Homeless Persons Shelter.

While this event was momentous, it was also very cheeky and provocative. Many of the invited parliamentary member were amused and sent telegrams of support and bunches of flowers. Many others accepted the 'invitation to be present at the opening' as 'happy to be a squatter' for the day. The day was a merry occasion.

But not without a drama. A pregnant woman was in labour but wanted to be present for the opening and would not go to hospital just yet. Guests were arriving and I was terrified she would deliver right there at the function. No coaxing would convince her to go to hospital. The baby was about to be born when she finally agreed to leave – but it was too late, baby was coming. I panicked and tried to drag her to her feet, but she could no longer walk. All she could do was waddle side-on like a crab up to the car. Then she could not get in. I was in a mad sweat. Meeting politicians and playing midwife at the same time was not on the agenda. Finally, with the help of others, I pushed and squeezed her into the front seat, her legs spreadeagled and almost hanging out the window. She got to the hospital just in time – it was a girl.

The official opening was a hoot but this outrageous manoeuvre proved to be more than the government was prepared to tolerate.

*

Our years of political agitation – squatting in our women's refuge at Ovingham;, raising issues of discrimination of women and the plight of sexually abused children;, setting up Kelly's Kids Shelter for homeless street kids; a rape crisis centre; support for a 'rape in marriage' clause to the Rape Act; and finally taking over a government mansion for homeless families; plus many more instances of raising hell via publicity from the media about many issues of women and children – were too much political embarrassment for them.

The government set about 'underhandedly collecting information and 'evidence of misdeeds' sufficient to justify them withdrawing our grant monies.

None of these statements were investigated. They were taken as verbatim truths. It gave a frustrated government reasons for withdrawing funds from shelters, in particular Naomi. They wanted us out. I was a thorn in their side. They did not want to deal with issues I was raising and, more to the point, they were probably trying to slur my credentials and quash a possible political threat, because I was being encouraged to stand as an independent candidate on a platform against domestic violence in the coming elections.

In 1982 at the beginning of our funding year, the state government withdrew funding from our shelter. We battled on for as long as our holding money lasted and then a little longer still. Publicity about our impending doom resulted in promises of financial support from businesses that could enable us to continue. We were torn and considered battling on but we had grown weary, over-worked, worn-out: we accepted the situation.

Tired of fighting on all fronts and exhausted from years of battling with issues, I decided to accept the closure. It was a sad time but I wear the political grumblings as a badge of honour. We women at Naomi must have been effective, for them to be so desperate.

Naomi Women's Shelter closed in 1983.

Other shelters also had their problems. The early women's shelter movement had been created by honourable, militant, like-minded women, but the ensuing, bitter, internal battles and takeovers severely damaged their credibility. Where there is money, there is always someone ready for mischief. The reputations of women's shelters in general were severely damaged by these conflicts. The women's movement also suffered. Such is the treachery of politics! And it has always been our women's history/herstory for feisty women to be pilloried.

A war-weary and embattled woman friend, a defeated, always ethically-minded southern shelter operative, later commiserated with me quietly. 'Annette, we paid a very high price, didn't we?'

5

1982–1994: My Own Separation and Struggle for Recovery

My children had all left home by this time, finding their own ways in the world, and I still lived at home. After Naomi closed, I had the opportunity to acquire a property that was registered as a guesthouse. It was a big, two-storey building, complete with caretaker's flat. I established it as an accommodation place for young adults with psychiatric problems and employed a small staff. We took in young adults with schizophrenia, some damaged by drugs or sexual abuse or family violence and other assorted dysfunctions, maladies and illnesses.

At home, life became increasingly violent. After one such episode, I moved out into the caretaker's flat. Mack kept calling me, pleading and pledging to do something about his behaviour. I acquiesced and accompanied him when he sought help.

'Why have you come to see me?' the psychiatrist asked Mack

'My wife has left me,' was his answer.

'And why do you think she has left you?' An obvious question, I thought

Mack prattled on about work and stress while I said nothing and wasn't asked anything.

'I think I drink too much and get angry,' admitted Mack with a morose hang-dog whimper.

A bit more small talk happened.

'You are a passive-aggressive. I know a passive-aggressive when I see one,' the psychiatrist said.

Passive? how wrong can this bloke be?

'And what about hobbies?' the professional asked.

Mack said he liked to sail. What a load of rubbish, I thought. Mack had not ever sailed in all the time I knew him. My father's flat-bottomed fishing boat floating about in the calm waters of Spencer Gulf could not in the wildest fantasies be called 'sailing'. But the doctor took up the cudgel and gave a fine oration on his own sailing skills and adventures.

'Yes, I would like a yacht,' said Mack.

'I think you should get a yacht and spend time sailing,' advised the doctor.

Oh, this is great! was all I could think. So we deal with bad behaviour and violence by getting him to spend his money on a yacht.

Consequently, Mack cashed in all the money he had from his super and bought a yacht. I kept my word and returned to live at home with him. We sailed a few times. Our sorties were reckless, as we were so lacking in sailing skills that they bordered on suicide missions and on more than one occasion we got close to drowning. The expensive yacht ran out of mooring fees. It was a financial disaster, leaving us with a debt that I later had to deal with. It solved nothing in our relationship and the violence continued. I procrastinated in my endeavour to separate and moved in and out of home for the next few years.

*

By the end of 1989, silent warning bells were again tolling for me but as usual I was still deaf and blind to them.

One evening I was at home and was caught off-guard with no time to flee. The violence in Mack had reached flashpoint again. He moved from verbal warnings to a surprise attack. I found myself trapped in the corner of the room. With sudden and unprovoked aggression, he fired his closed fist at my head. It connected and split open a previous injury. I moved slightly aside as he launched his next punch and he screamed in pain as his fist connected not with my head but with the wall. He fractured his right metacarpus. His hand was clearly broken.

'Drive me to the hospital,' he moaned as he leant over in pain, holding his arm.

'Drive yourself!' I spat at him in caustic defiance as I held my bleeding open wound.

A few days later, I accompanied him to his work Christmas party and listened to his humorous quibbling explanation of how he broke his hand. Something snapped in my brain and I could stand their laughter no longer. 'No, you didn't,' I broke in. 'You broke it hurling a punch at me.'

Well, the earth fell in. Faces in the room grimaced and conversations stopped mid-sentence. Wine glasses were poised in mid-flight and the room fell silent. I could hardly believe I had said that. All eyes were turned my way. I was stunned and felt the shock of my own surprising outburst. The audience stared at me in disbelief.

I was surprised myself, but I was indifferent to all their gawking. I felt nothing. I was calm and serene. I simply stood there with a blank face. The cover-ups, the lies, were over and the Secret Families Act was secret no more! I was past hope, past pretending and past caring.

But that in itself did not send me out of his evil orbit.

*

I went home with him and quivered behind the blue haze of my emotional dilemma. I had had enough, but my head was in a muddle. I could not fathom out what to do next. I was confused and unable to make any moves, let alone the right one. I worried about our crippling debts.

Over the next days I kept apologising to my sister, to my staff. 'Sorry, sorry, for not… Sorry for bothering you… Sorry.'

Should I go or stay? What should I do? What day should I go? I had no idea what I was doing or saying.

Mack prowled around the house all night every night, banging doors, playing loud music, walking into my room and switching on the light and switching it off again. Every day I struggled to go to work. I finally got a locksmith to put a lock on my door. Why did I bother? Why didn't I just leave and go back to my caretaker's flat? I'll never know.

When he saw my locked door, all hell erupted with the intensity of an operatic tragedy. Evil glared me in the face.

'I'll chop the fucking door down!' He was screaming as he stormed out of the house in search of an axe.

An axe! Oh no, was death again staring at me? I am getting too old for this. Run, my inner voice screamed. Dressed only in my nightgown and with no shoes, I grabbed the car keys off the entrance table and stealthily tiptoed out of the house.

I was two steps along the veranda when he appeared with the long-handled axe. He blocked my path. I was trapped. With a taunted twisting face, he quick paced towards me raising the axe above his head as if to strike. He approached close. My heart jumped and my head raced. You fool…fool. I was too late – frozen in fear. Would death by axe hurt? Stay calm, whispered my inner voice. I forced a tranquil calm ripple to flow over me. I knew without a doubt that if I panicked and ran, his rage would escalate, he would chase me, catch me and there would be a bloodbath.

His face was twisted with fury. Face to face, we eyed each other. I was watching the poised head of a bobbing snake. In the seconds that ticked by, I worked out a mental picture of where the axe would swing on its downward path. While the axe was falling to the right, I could jump to the left. During the seconds that took him to recover, I could rush past him and cover the few metres to the car. I don't remember feeling panic or fear in those seconds. My thoughts were icy calm. My life was at stake. Panic could come later, after the storm.

That is how it happened. I ran to the car.

He recovered quickly and was right behind me screaming, 'I'll kill you, you fucking bitch. I'll kill you.'

I reached the car, threw myself in and locked the door. I turned the key. It didn't start. He's going to smash his way in! It was time to pray. 'Please God, save my life,' a selfish, bargaining plea. 'I promise, I will leave and never put my life in danger again, ever again.' I repeated this mantra over and over as I kept turning the key. 'Please God, please save my life.'

Mack's raging distorted face was at the window. He pulled at the door but it didn't move and the car was squeezed too close to the fence for him to raise the axe. He moved to the front bonnet and raised the axe, all the time threatening and abusing. He was a monster, an angry unrecognisable monster – a picture I have never been able to remove from my memory.

Miraculously, the car sprang to life and I screeched backwards out of the driveway, hoping that there was no car coming along the road. Stunned but composed, I turned on the cassette player. I turned and heard the axe smashing into the door of the house. Pavarotti softly sang 'O Sole Mio' as I peacefully let the car take me away from the insanity – into the next insanity of my mind.

I do not know where I drove or for how long, or when I parked, but it was daylight when I woke up. I looked around and saw people walking past the car. I was in a big shopping centre car park in my flimsy nightdress.

The sun was well risen and he should be at work. I drove back to the house and cautiously surveyed the scene. The doors had been smashed to pieces. I stepped over the rubble on high alert, collected some clothing and personal belongings, left the car in the drive and took the campervan.

I drove to the house of my eldest daughter, who was interstate for work. I had her house keys. I switched the roller door to open, parked the van in her carport and nestled down into a hypnotic, blue haze. Traumatised, shivering in disbelief, the scene replayed itself in my mind for more than a week.

'Thank you, heavenly Father.' I finally remembered to give thanks for my life. Once again, I had escaped and this time I was going to keep my promise. I was never going back. I stayed locked in my van in my daughter's car port for a week too afraid to venture out – even into her house.

I then settled into the caretaker's flat at work. I had survived and carried on, in my own sanguine way, as though nothing untoward had happened. Insanity and madness sneaked in and stayed with me.

*

Two years passed. I was still living in the caretaker's flat. I slowly fell apart. My staff told me so. I did not function well any more, even though I tried to convince myself I was all right. Household and business debts were mounting and years of unpaid council rates were threatening closure. Mortgages failed, maintenance was not done and I fell into a dysfunctional stupor. I relied on others.

Mack appeared at times, mostly drunk and rowdy and Ron, who was one of my employees and a nine-year-dry recovering alcoholic, took me aside one day and said, 'Annette, you need help.' He took me off to his Alcoholics Anonymous meetings even though it was not me who was the alcoholic. I was amazed at his insight into my dysfunctional behaviour. I went to the Al Anon meetings which supported spouses and families of persons with drinking problems and I learnt a lot from these organised women. I felt I had friends.

It gave me a lot to think about. I had attended quite a few of their meetings before I actually heard their message: 'just be honest'. It was from them that I learnt that I needed to take care of myself. 'Tell yourself how it really is, as it is, and be honest with yourself' echoed in my ears from then on.

I had to face the facts. I could not make decisions, I could not manage the financial burdens or the rowdy, disturbed residents. I began to experience minor illnesses. It was time to quit and take care of myself, so I disposed of the guest house and moved back into our home, which Mack had wrecked and abandoned. I repaired what I could and rescued the yacht from the marina, hoping to save some of the assets.

*

I had never wanted to leave my Adelaide home. I clung to it like it was my refuge. I had so much of my life invested in it. I had saved all the money I earned while working in Western Australia and had used it as a deposit for the house. It was a lovely old bluestone house with solid, thick walls, huge rooms with ornate ceilings and beautifully crafted fireplaces. It was a big house by the standards I was used to.

Each week that I worked in the factories, I spent my meagre 'pocket money' earnings on rickety old Edwardian furniture from op shops. It was unwanted and inexpensive and I spent hours restoring, scrubbing and scraping at hard crusted paint, then sanding and polishing to expose the beautiful red colour of the cedar. I loved each piece. Mack hated all the 'old mausoleum junk' but he made no attempt to choose something else for the house.

The Family Court forced me to sell my home and when it came to a property settlement, suddenly my old junk became valuable antiques. I had to liquidate my beloved possessions and share the money with the man who had shamed me when I was a child and who had continued to bash and abuse me for thirty years, a man who cheated and lied to my parents, who abused my children. The fact that he benefited when the court took away all my possessions was just another example of his power to destroy whatever I treasured. Women fear losing all they hold dear when they decide to leave, and I was no different.

*

Then my family splintered apart. Domestic violence has a way of weaving its way across family lines. A feud involving siblings, cousins, aunts erupted and my heart broke. We were never again to be fully reunited.

*

So I began to journey on a very rocky road. My business wound up. Debt management was put in place and I moved out to the country, where I bought a run-down, old wooden schoolhouse for a song. I set up in a camping sort of way. Luckily, I had water and electricity. There was a rough, functioning kitchen with hot water and showers and plenty of land around.

I went nowhere, saw no one and tried to piece together what had happened. I had no interest in what was occurring outside my four walls. It is hard to explain or describe the desolate feeling brought on by loss. I knew I needed help but had no idea where I could find any.

During the early and mid-1990s my emotional suffering escalated. I sat and cried often and had long bouts of depression that lasted for days, weeks, months. Feelings of shame and guilt were rising and stayed ever present. How could this be happening to me? What is it that is happening? How did I get to this state? I could not understand why I felt so angry and revengeful.

I went to see a lawyer and could not tell her why I was there. Words would not come. I cried hysterically in her office and could offer no explanation.

'You don't need a lawyer,' she said patiently. 'You need a psychiatrist.'

Where do you find psychiatrists? Especially when you are out of control and out of your mind? Besides, I had had my fill of psychiatrists. I had no need of another yacht.

*

Advertised in the local paper one day was a 'support group for victims of abuse' in a country town not so far from me. I had come to realise that I was indeed a victim of abuse and decided to go and see what help was on offer.

Meekly and with downcast eyes, I crept to an empty chair. I spoke to no one. I looked dowdy. My hair had not been cut for months and the boots I was wearing were scuffed and worn, my clothes shabby, and I needed new ones. I looked like all the other grim-faced, impoverished women sitting there in a semicircle, waiting for the convenor to arrive. There were twelve of us, all forlorn and forsaken, wrecks of human beings. As I sat grimly with my head down, his words came back to me: 'You're nothing without me... I made you what you are...' I thought, yes, all my years with him have brought me to this. I am a scabby, worthless nothing. Yes, I am now what you made me. Your years of intimidation, violence, threats and abuse turned me into this human wreck.

The convenor arrived. In a cheery and upbeat voice, she began by telling us about her overseas trip. She went on and on. Then she introduced a game reminiscent of the 1960s Tupperware party games. I watched her in bewilderment as she introduced a 'pass the parcel' children's game. I passed at my turn to open the parcel. As each woman unwrapped the layers of paper, the look on the 'lucky' woman's face as an unwanted gimcrack souvenir, a miniature Eiffel Tower, fell unto her lap told it all. I watched mystified as the convenor got the women to bop a balloon around for a second game.

When a third game started, I thought, 'Oh hell, I must be at the wrong meeting,' and stood up to leave.

Red-shot eyes looked at me. My move to go had interrupted the proceedings.

'Sorry, but I thought this was a domestic violence support group.'

'Why, yes, it is.'

I looked around at the women. It couldn't be with such shenanigans going on, surely not? The bedraggled women looked back. Yes. They certainly looked like survivors of abuse.

'Are you all victims of domestic violence?' as if I needed to ask.

No one said anything. The women's eyes looked from me to the convenor and she glared at me.

'Well,' I said, raising my arm, 'I am a victim of domestic violence,' there I actually said it, and the uncomfortable-looking women all slowly raised their arms too. I felt the power and comfort of my raised hand as the other women slowly joined me.

'So, if this is a domestic violence support group and we are all victims, and we've been here for one hour, why haven't I heard one word about domestic violence?'

'Oh no, we don't talk about violence here. We're not here to make each other miserable. We play games to make us happy.'

I looked at all the downcast, grim, unsmiling women with raised hands and turned to the convenor. 'You're a disgrace!' I said, my one hand still raised and the other pointing a finger straight at her.

I stood, momentarily considering my next move. Should I say more? Should I attempt to direct this support group? The situation seemed outrageous to me. A government-funded support program run by fools. I swallowed, realising that I was in no fit state to intervene. I needed help myself and had not the strength to take on an issue. I simply walked out.

*

I went back to my safe haven at the schoolhouse and decided I would have to find my own way to recovery. My eldest daughter and I were, luckily for me, in constant contact. She had moved to Sydney as a journalist and writer and encouraged me to start writing. I am not a writer and writing does not come easily to me but it seemed like a good idea. So I tried.

'Keep it simple' was the AA motto. 'One day at a time. Tell the truth and get real.'.

Real…but what is real? There were only secrets.

Words did not come. Only questions that haunted me and circled around in my brain. What had happened? I couldn't remember. Why am I here? Where are my children, grandchildren? I could not remember my children's birthdays or their birthday parties or any other events in their lives. I couldn't remember any of our Christmases nor my own birthday celebrations. I could not remember what I did with them. I know we ate meals, but what sort of food did I cook for them? I know they wore clothes, but I couldn't remember what size they wore at what age. I didn't remember buying them clothes and when I heard a neighbour say, 'When my son was twelve he was in the footy team,' I burst into a flood of tears, because I couldn't remember what my children did at different ages.

I cried a lot. I felt weak and ill, but had nothing physically wrong with me. Feelings of guilt and shame, loss and grief threatened to drown me. The sound of a slamming door, the smell of alcohol, voices raised in anger or the sight of a smashed building would send tremors through my body and make me feel afraid.

'Keep it simple.'

'One day at a time.'

How many days would this go on? I wanted to quit.

I heard Ron's kind, patient voice: 'It takes time. Be patient and remember the twelve steps every day.'

All I wanted was for the shame and horror to be over with. I wanted to get on with a life. AA is not for everyone, but the program helped me. It gave me a simple system to follow while I was at my lowest ebb.

*

'Write,' encouraged my daughter's voice.

I got together writing paper and pens, but still the words would not come. Mmy mind would not let me remember. So I took to the garden. I liked living in the country. I liked my distant farm neighbours and their generous friendship – they plied me with gifts of jams and fresh fruit. Out in the garden, or while caring for wounded animals, I kept thinking and trying to bring some sort of memory back.

For a while, nothing would come to mind. I fed the rescued kangaroos, and motherless baby parrots. Time came to have an elusive quality.

However, one day as I was planting a tree, a flash of something urgent came into my head and I ran inside and wrote down just exactly what I had seen. I wrote I remember when…it was a secret and I could not tell…but, I could write it down. My breakthrough! I wrote frantically. From then on, every time I had a glimpse of an event, I would drop everything and write it down. There was no sequence to the memories. I continued life and kept adding to these spasmodic writings for weeks, maybe months. I was oblivious of the passing of time. Then just as suddenly, I stopped writing and put the papers aside.

*

I was drained but a great weight had lifted. Three or more months went by and one day I took out the writings to read back what I had written. Was that me I had written about? My insides churned and turned to jelly. Ron had warned me that I might not feel like I could handle what I unearthed, but he drummed in the mantra, 'Just get real. Stop the rot. Stop hiding behind the secret.' And so I ploughed on to unearth more reality.

Reality hit hard. I couldn't believe what I had written down about myself and my children and our life in violence. I was afraid of what I was realising. I spiralled down again in despair as the true picture of my past life emerged and I allowed the pain to come. How could I have been so stupid? How could our lives have become the tragedy of now?

There was no turning back. I continued to write, searching, searching, and questioning the truth of everything. My inner secrets were escaping. It got worse and worse and hard to deal with and to make sense of. Just when I thought I had a clear picture, more stories crept in and added more horrific facts. The 'I remember…' scribbles forced me to face a painful reality. I, Annette Willcox, defender of women victims of violence, was myself a victim. At the same time as I was working at the women's shelters supporting women and children and helping them to escape violence, I was returning home night after night to face abuse and indignity and, worse, was not seeing that my own children were being violated. My children carry on the family secret: a lifelong legacy of secret abuse. I see so clearly now the bitter legacy they must suffer and it shames and humiliates me.

Mistreatment in my home was not restricted to my children and me. My sisters who came to my home under my care did not escape either. Where there is abuse in the home, all who live or come near there, suffer the vibrating effects – there is no escape.

*

In 1994, I was called to a pre-divorce conference. Because I had been remembering more and more 'incidents' that happened in my family, memories of things said confirmed what had been happening when I was not at home. I was very upset, fuming mad, frustrated and still powerless. I stormed into the counselling room. The counsellor sat opposite where Mack was sitting waiting and I stood with clenched fist.

'Sit down, Mrs Elliot,' the counsellor said.

Bugger you! I thought, and deliberately refused to sit down. I stood tall for the first time, mad and courageous, pointing at my ex-husband, as I clearly spat out the rushing words from my mouth.

With new-found memories rushing around my head, of him pocking the children's gums, of him thumbnailing their ears, of my screams the children heard and assaults they witnessed, of seeing the children quiver in fear. His words 'Nothing happened, you weren't hurt,' when all the time, something did happen and we were hurt.

I let fly my pent-up anger and raised my voice for all to hear. 'I know what you did to the children. I know what you did to us!'

He said nothing.

I kept my voice high, repeating my mantra.

Finally, he could stand it no longer. 'Liar. You're a liar,' he cried in expected response. 'You are a liar,' he repeated. 'Nothing happened, you are a liar.'

'Oh no. No, you can't use that one on me any more. I know what you did. We were hurt and it did happen. I know what you did. I know what I know, and I know what you did...' I went on and on repeating my mantra, announcing his violence towards me, and the children.

The counsellor did not intervene. He had no control of the session and looked on with a red, embarrassed face. I ignored him. Then a miracle happened. Mack cried. He cried! Tears ran down his face. I was shocked. But I felt no sympathy, no remorse. I was cold and calm. He actually cried tears! I felt a surge of renewed power. Without further words, he ran out of the room – it was his time to run in tears. 'Yes!' I said to myself. 'Yes!'

As I looked back at the perplexed and astounded counsellor's face, Mack's own words came back racing to me and I said to him, 'Liars – they all cry when they're found out.'

Epilogue

I have ended my personal story at the point of my growing strength and awareness. Because of the reasons for long-term violence/abuse, the saga can be enduring and tedious and recovery can extend for many years, so the story can take on a long life. As I progressed to a new me, I found it was necessary to move on and follow various lines of approach to recording domestic violence issues from what I have learned. There are abundant avenues and I continue to write from another perspective.

I wrote *Secret Secrets* post-separation during a dark, long and traumatic period of my life. It was part therapy, part anger and part loss and grief that drove me. And it was part research to discover how and why my life was in such a mess long after divorce and what happens to women, and children and what are the long-term consequences for families who live with domestic violence. It is not pretty. The legacy of my research is that I have achieved and grasped enormous truth and wisdom. I have learned a lot. In the future I will continue the narrative and I look forward to recording the murky shadows of domestic violence and how it operates.

Domestic violence is a crime, a slow hideous, pernicious and duplicitous serious crime without due criminal legislation to bring perpetrators to account for the massive damage they inflict on humanity. No Domestic Violence is my passion and it is my mission to continue to advocate for politicians to enact appropriate, fit-for-purpose legislation to make domestic violence a criminal offence under the Criminal Law Consolidation Act 1935.

On a personal note, I have finally gained peace and happiness with close-by sisters and caring daughter. I have relocated in a sea change, taking grace and making new friends and loving every space and minute of it. With a new life, I have years of brightness and productive future ahead of me.

Acknowledgements

To all the women who told me their stories. I thank them for their trust and sharing their secrets. I hope they will help other women.

To Lannie Kinnimart, who welcomed me to her kitchen and patiently listened to my story. She was first to read my work and gave me advice I did not like. Nevertheless, I pursued her advice and I am glad I did.

To Nan Berrett from Word Solutions, who cast her talented eye and followed with gentle manipulation of my choice of some words. We shared coffee and she boosted my confidence to carry on.

To Paul Heywood Smith QC, whose legal opinion was helpful and gratifying. His support was necessary and much appreciated. My book could not have proceeded to conclusion without his help. I thank him immensely.

To my dear sister Diane Ellis, who helped me unravel unpldeasant memoies and put them into place, and to my dear sister Elizabeth Elliot, who was on hand to correct my computer when I pressed the wrong buttons – my love and gratitude.

Domestic violence is not a nice subject, and in conversation many publishers declare that it would not 'fit their criteria' and others would be shy to even read a manuscript. Therefore I must acknowledge Stephen Matthews of Ginninderra Press, who took the time and accepted my work for publication. I thank him for his faith and commitment.

And especially, I must acknowledge and honour my daughter Jacqueline Willcox. She was with me in the beginning, courageously standing firm at the 'barricades', squatting in a vacant scary house that became SA's first women's shelter. And she was with me in support and encouragement to the last page of writing this book. With love and gratitude, I owe her much and thank her for her faith in me.

Resources

Books

Anne Summers, *Ducks on the Pond*, 1999
Annette Willcox, *The Naomi Report*, 1977

Contacts

Campaign for legislation to make domestic violence a criminal offence

No Domestic Violence, email annettee246@outlook.com

Child help national child abuse hotline
1800 422 4453

1800RESPECT
1800 737 732
24-hour national sexual assault, family and domestic violence counselling line for any Australian who has experienced, or is at risk of, family and domestic violence and/or sexual assault.

Lifeline
13 11 14
Lifeline has a national number which can help put you in contact with a crisis service in your state.

Police and Ambulance
000

Translating and Interpreting Service
131 450
Gain free access to a telephone or onsite interpreter in your own language.

Suicide Call Back Service
1300 659 467
Free counselling 24/7, whether you're feeling suicidal, are worried about someone else, or have lost someone to suicide.

Kids helpline
1800 551 800
Free, private and confidential, telephone and online counselling service specifically for young people aged between 5 and 25 in Australia.

Australian Childhood Foundation
1800 176 453
Counselling for children and young people affected by abuse.

Relationships Australia
1300 364 277
Support groups and counselling on relationships, and for abusive and abused partners.

Blue Knot Foundation
1300 657 380
(9 a.m.–5 p.m.)
Telephone counselling for adult survivors of childhood trauma, their friends, family and the health care professionals who support them.

National Disability Abuse and Neglect Hotline
1800 880 052
An Australia-wide telephone hotline for reporting abuse and neglect of people with disability.

Recommended domestic violence abuse programs providing services for men

Mensline Australia
1300 789 978
24/7 telephone and online support and information service for Australian men. Supports men and boys who are dealing with family and relationship difficulties.

9 781760 417987